INSIDE THE UNITED NATIONS

a critical look at the UN

D0616611

by Steve Bonta

THE JOHN BIRCH SOCIETY
Appleton, Wisconsin

Front cover photo by Bob Krist/Corbis
Back cover photo by Reuters NewMedia Inc./Corbis

Second Printing

Published by
THE JOHN BIRCH SOCIETY
Post Office Box 8040
Appleton, Wisconsin 54912
www.jbs.org

Printed in the United States of America
LC Control Number
2003100241
ISBN: 1-881919-08-0

"The great rule of conduct for us, in regard to foreign nations is, in extending our commercial relations, to have with them as little political connection as possible … It is our true policy to steer clear of permanent alliance with any portion of the foreign world."

George Washington,
Farewell Address

Contents

Introduction

To most of us, the United Nations symbolizes the quest for world peace. Yet since the UN's founding more than 50 years ago, world peace has remained elusive. We have seen wars in Korea, Vietnam, the Middle East, the Balkans, and across much of Africa and Latin America. Millions of innocents have been slaughtered in horrific genocides from Cambodia to Rwanda. We have witnessed an unprecedented buildup of weapons so deadly that millions of lives can be snuffed out with the push of a button. More recently, we have seen international terrorism claim thousands of lives on American soil on one terrible day. We are now engaged in yet another war, the struggle against international terrorism which has already taken many lives and may be prolonged for many years. The era of the United Nations has not, by any stretch of the imagination, been a peaceful one.

Why hasn't the United Nations lived up to its billing? Defenders of the United Nations insist that the catastrophes in recent world history have occurred not because of the UN, but in spite of it. A stronger and more efficient United Nations, they argue, would certainly have the power to prevent such calamities from happening in the future.

But in truth, world peace is only one of several arguments used to justify the UN's existence. The United Nations has also been promoted as a means of eradicating world poverty, improving world health standards, and protecting the global environment, to name just three familiar issues. None of these justifications, however, answers the most important question about the United Nations: What is its real purpose?

This book will show that the ultimate goal behind the United Nations system is the creation of a single world government, the consequences of which would be devastating both for America as a whole and for Americans individually. Loss of national sovereignty under any global regime would reduce the United States of America to a dependent fiefdom, unable to exercise its authority independently in military, legal, judicial, financial, or social affairs. Individually, Americans would become "global citizens" under the final authority of a global government. The Declaration of Independence and the U.S. Constitution would become irrelevant, along with the individual, God-given rights they proclaim and protect.

Many Americans might find such scenarios far-fetched. Much of the public support the United Nations enjoyed in its early years has dwindled, but most Americans still do not regard the UN as a genuine threat. A large number of

Americans believe that the glass and steel architecture of the UN Secretariat in New York City harbors nothing more sinister than inept, harmless bureaucrats and diplomats trying to bring about world peace through impractical, misguided methods. In reality, as this book will show, the United Nations system was created by scheming men hostile to the United States and its tradition of limited government. The UN is also promoted by misleading and even deliberately deceptive language, and is based on false and dangerous principles. For these reasons, the bureaucracy headquartered on the East River poses a very serious threat to the United States.

This book will focus on certain basic facts and principles relating to the most commonly held perceptions about the UN. For example, since most people think about the UN primarily as an organization dedicated to preventing war, much of the book deals with the UN in relation to the question of war and peace. On the other hand, many of the UN's lesser-known activities — in areas like global environmentalism, abortion, and the so-called "new world religion" — will not be treated in this book in any detail. This is to preserve simplicity and brevity in what is intended to be a brief introduction to a vast and complicated subject.

As time passes, some of the historical events described in this book may seem less and less relevant. Some, like the situation in the Middle East, may change. But the basic principles pertaining to the United Nations and to the question of world government will not. For this reason, this book is first and foremost about principles. It is hoped that even readers years into the future, when the events and actors described in these pages have become history, will still be able to discern the principles and apply them to events in their own time.

This book explains the growing danger posed by U.S. membership in the United Nations. It has been written to persuade a sleeping America that entanglement with the United Nations is one of the deadliest, most subtle threats to independence that our country has ever faced — in large part because so few recognize the danger. As a very modest introduction to the UN, this book is intended to encourage the reader to learn more about the United Nations system from in-depth works on the subject. Finally, this book proposes a solution to the UN problem as well as a vision of an alternative future world where freedom, independence, and relative peace will flourish without the overseership of the United Nations or any other comparable international organization.

1
The Citizen and the Soldiers

On the morning of August 25th, 1944, a strange drama was unfolding outside the high iron gates of the secluded Georgetown estate known as Dumbarton Oaks. On that warm late summer morning, a man claiming to represent the America First movement and the interests of "American nationalists" was arguing heatedly with military police assigned to guard the gates, demanding access to the international conference taking place inside. For several days, delegates from the governments of three world powers — the United States, Great Britain, and the Soviet Union — had been meeting there under a cloak of secrecy. Congress had been told little more than that the men meeting at Dumbarton Oaks were laying plans for a postwar security arrangement, an organization that would help prevent future world wars. Even the press had been excluded from the proceedings, except for a meaningless opening-day ceremony.

Members of the media, angry at being denied access to this obviously important conference, and tired of waiting outside the imposing gates with nothing to do, gathered around the flamboyant America Firster as the man stated his case to the indifferent soldiers. Days earlier, he insisted, he had sent a telegraph to Cordell Hull, President Franklin Roosevelt's Secretary of State, warning that, unless Americanist senators were admitted to the conference, he would come himself to represent the "millions of inarticulate nationalists who are determined that there shall be no super state and no world police force after this war." Since Secretary Hull had ignored his request, he was now presenting himself in person.

However, the soldiers prevented him from entering. The American delegation, made up mostly of Roosevelt administration officials, had no intention of allowing a so-called "isolationist" to participate in their semisecret gathering. The America Firster eventually gave up in disgust and left. But the episode attracted a lot of press coverage, prompting many Americans to wonder what *was* taking place at Dumbarton Oaks.

Well should Americans have taken notice. However, in the summer of 1944, the public's attention was riveted on events in Europe and Asia. The Allied forces, successful on the beaches of Normandy in June, were now advancing against Hitler's armies in France. In the Pacific, recent lopsided American victories against the Japanese at Saipan and Tinian in the Marshall Islands suggested that victory over

Japan was close at hand. In contrast to the drama of World War II, the drab spectacle of obscure officials in dull suits meeting in an out-of-the-way corner of Washington was of little interest to much of the public. Most of the conference participants — men like Alger Hiss, Lawrence Duggan, Noel Field, and Victor Perlo — weren't household names in the days when the likes of Douglas MacArthur, George Patton, and Jimmy Doolittle dominated the headlines.

What Americans didn't know in August of 1944 was that many of the members of the American delegation at Dumbarton Oaks were either Communists or strong Communist sympathizers. A number of them, including the now-notorious Alger Hiss, who served as secretary for the conference, were eventually unmasked as spies and traitors. They deplored America's system of free enterprise that had produced the greatest prosperity and the largest middle class the world had ever seen. Coming mostly from upper-crust northeastern families and flaunting Ivy League diplomas, they saw America, and Americans, as backward and isolationist, and were determined to exploit the chaos of world war to remake America — and the world — in their own image.

A few well-informed Americans, most notably the former members of the America First movement, were aware of the intentions of the Dumbarton Oaks group. On August 23rd, a representative of the America Firsters — the same individual who tried to crash the gates at Dumbarton Oaks two days later — distributed among members of Congress and the media a letter he had sent to Secretary of State Cordell Hull. In the letter, he accused the Roosevelt administration of conducting the conference in a manner "foreign to our American tradition," because of the total exclusion of both the press and Congress. The letter claimed that the conference, though officially nonpartisan, served only a single set of interests — those of the "internationalists." The letter even accused the State Department of attempting to violate the Constitution. The Roosevelt administration had set up a conference on American soil filled with foreigners, the letter continued, and was sharing facts with agents of the British and Soviet governments that it was keeping secret from Americans — and then using soldiers to keep the American people out. Finally, the letter accused the government of using the cover of war to drag the United States into a new League of Nations.

The accusations were right on target. The delegates at the conference were, as charged, drawing up plans for a new global "security" organization to replace the failing League of Nations. They worked in secret because they knew that the American people, and a majority of their representatives in Congress, would never approve the project. They intended that the new international institution they were creating be at first only a loose collective of the world's nations working together to promote "world order." In time, they expected, the organization would grow in both prestige and power, as sovereign nations got used to deferring to its authority. In the end, they expected, their organization would become a genuine world government. They decided to call the new organization the United Nations.

The Dumbarton Oaks blueprint for the United Nations called for taking "effective collective measures for the prevention and removal of threats to the peace and the suppression of acts of aggression," and for creating "a center for harmonizing the actions of nations in the achievement of these common ends." Put simply, the United Nations was to be a mechanism for the entire world to gang up on any country thought to be a threat. The document also provided for "international cooperation in the solution of international economic, social, and other humanitarian problems." This deliberately vague language meant that the UN was to use the power of government internationally to target social, financial, and economic ills.

The same internationalists who created the United Nations also gave us other international organizations: The IMF, or International Monetary Fund, for control of international finance; the World Bank, to oversee a permanent transfer of wealth from rich to poor nations; and regional security organizations like the North Atlantic Treaty Organization (NATO). But the United Nations was to be the nerve center for all of them, coordinating the growth of a whole host of international organizations into bona fide instruments of world government.

The conferees at Dumbarton Oaks planned a world ruled and managed by them, using any means possible. But they also understood that the world government or "new world order" they sought could not be achieved in a single blow. Instead, their plans called for acquiring power gradually and, above all, creating at least the appearance of popular support. The United Nations, by itself a paper tiger, was a means to that end, because it was designed to be a base upon which the new world order could be constructed, plank by plank, across several generations.

Almost 30 years after the founding of the UN, Columbia University political science professor and veteran State Department functionary Richard Gardner, writing in the April 1974 issue of *Foreign Affairs* magazine, reminded readers of the long-term recipe for world government:

If instant world government... [does] not provide the answers, what hope for progress is there?... [T]he "house of world order" will have to be built from the bottom up rather than the top down. It will look like a great "booming, buzzing confusion," to use William James' famous description of reality, but an end run around national sovereignty, eroding it piece by piece, will accomplish much more than the old-fashioned frontal assault... [F]or political as well as administrative reasons, some of these specialized arrangements should be brought into an appropriate relationship with the central institutions of the UN system.

But few Americans in 1944 anticipated the long-term consequences of a UN-centered new world order. The UN was billed as a forum for negotiating postwar peace agreements and other treaties, not as an embryonic world government. The United Nations organization came into being on October 24, 1945, three months after 50 countries, including the United States, first signed and then formally ratified the United Nations Charter. In the U.S. Senate, only two votes were cast against it. The construction of the "house of world order" — to use Richard Gardner's terminology — was underway.

2
Sovereignty

America is surrendering its sovereignty to a world government. Hooray.
— Cover of *The New Republic,* January 17, 2000, referring to an article by Robert Wright.

Anybody who reads major national news magazines and newspapers these days will eventually come across articles and op-ed pieces like the one written by Robert Wright for *The New Republic* in January 2000. The article, entitled "Continental Drift," told readers that "world government is coming. Deal with it." Wright admitted that, where world government is concerned, the "flaky" political fringe is right: World government really is on the way, but, he maintained, "it's a good idea." He argued that dramatic increases in international trade and information technology have broken down barriers and created a single global marketplace, making world government necessary. UN Secretary-General Kofi Annan has said, in a similar vein, that "every community needs rules. The international community needs them as much as a local community or district." And a *Wall Street Journal* article, on January 1, 2000, under the heading "A World Without a Country?," predicted that "the nation-state will undergo sharp limitations in its sovereignty" and will "have to dissolve into wider structures." The writer of the *Journal* article was careful to add that nation-states won't be completely abolished, at least in appearance, because "[people] need inspiration and some sort of spiritual uplift. That is why the trappings of the nation-state will be with us for a long time, although perhaps only as a kind of ceremonial show business."

Modern apologists for world government often argue that sovereign, independent nation-states are old-fashioned and encourage wars and financial instability. World government, we are told, will unite humanity under a single benevolent rule, leading to world peace and perpetual economic growth. According to this view, independent nations stubbornly defending their sovereignty are obstacles to this future golden age.

The concept of sovereignty, unfortunately, is poorly understood and little appreciated these days. Trade wars, financial crises, real and imaginary environmental problems, poverty, and warfare have all been blamed on national sovereignty. Modern opinion makers encourage Americans to view themselves as part of the "global community," and of having obligations to the world that transcend loyalty to their own country.

National sovereignty, however, is absolutely central to American liberty. When Thomas Jefferson penned the Declaration of Independence in 1776, he proclaimed the collective right of the American colonists to, in the Declaration's own words, "dissolve the Political Bands which have connected them with another, and to assume among the Powers of the Earth, a separate and equal Station." According to the Declaration, "the Laws of Nature and of Nature's God" entitled them to do so. The entire Declaration of Independence, with its list of truths, rights and grievances, rests upon this first premise, that any group of people — in this case, the American colonists — are justified by the laws of God, under certain circumstances, in declaring their independence from all other political powers and forming a new country. This new union of "free and independent states," Jefferson wrote in the final paragraph of the Declaration, would now have "full Power to levy War, conclude Peace, contract Alliances, establish Commerce, and to do all other Acts and Things which INDEPENDENT STATES, may of right do."

This condition, in which a people set up and maintain a government independent of all other earthly governments, is called *sovereignty*, and is virtually synonymous with *independence*. According to the great Dutch legal theorist Hugo Grotius, whose writings many of the Founding Fathers admired:

> That power is called sovereign whose actions are not subject to the legal control of another, so that they cannot be rendered void by the operation of another human will.

For America's Founders, sovereignty was a necessary precondition for liberty; without complete independence from the British crown, our Founding Fathers could never have produced our American Constitution, with its legacy of freedom and limited government. And just as sovereignty was essential for America to *obtain* her freedom, so today Americans can *retain* their freedom only if they preserve their precious sovereignty.

The God-given condition of sovereignty, then, allows people to join together as separate nations, to choose their mode of government, and to reap the abundant blessings of ordered, civilized existence. As conditions within one state become unendurable — because of war, tyrannical government, or environmental hardship — groups of people have historically migrated to new places and set up new states, or changed conditions in their own country by whatever means their circumstances demanded.

This, of course, is an oversimplified picture. In the real world, nations do not always conduct themselves according to just principles. Sovereignty isn't necessarily a permanent condition. It may be eroded or lost altogether, as strong nations prey upon the weak. History is full of examples of hard-won independence being lost, by conquest or by consent.

Loss of sovereignty by *conquest* is a familiar theme in world history. All of the well-known conquerors — men like Alexander the Great, Julius Caesar, Genghis Khan, Napoleon Bonaparte, Adolf Hitler, and many others — enlarged their power by militarily invading and conquering weaker nations. They are remembered chiefly for their brutality; Genghis Khan and his Mongol armies, for example, were known for putting to death every living inhabitant of many of the cities they conquered.

A nation may also lose all or part of its sovereignty by *consent*. This occurs when a nation, or its leaders, decides voluntarily to relinquish some of its freedom of self-determination and enter into an enforceable agreement with another nation. The agreement may take the form of a confederacy or other form of association of formerly independent nations, which unite under a new governmental authority. Countries like Switzerland and Italy came into being in this way. So did the United States, as the separate colonies united after independence under the original Articles of Confederation, and later strengthened that confederation into a "more perfect union" under the U.S. Constitution. The former American colonies decided that a union would be more advantageous than remaining as 13 completely separate, sovereign states. Separate, they might soon begin fighting each other, and would become easy prey for European powers. United, however, they could protect each other from foreign threats.

Partial loss of independence by consent may also occur when separate nations sign treaties, such as defensive alliances that require signatories to come to each other's aid if any member of the alliance is attacked by an outside power. The American Founders were very concerned that America might dilute her own independence by getting involved in alliances with overseas powers that would drag her into foreign wars having nothing to do with America's vital interests. President George Washington, in his Farewell Address, warned against such entangling foreign alliances, saying:

> Why quit our own to stand upon foreign ground? Why, by interweaving our destiny with that of any part of Europe, entangle our peace and prosperity in the toils of European ambition, rivalship, interest, humor, or caprice?

Washington and the Founders understood that the

United States of America, because of her favorable geography, had no need for dependence on the Old World. Besides being physically separated from Europe and its quarrels, America was and is blessed with a wonderful climate and a rich array of natural resources allowing her to be materially self-sufficient. The Founders also expected that, because of America's unique freedoms and the sturdy character of her people, she would soon be strong enough and prosperous enough to take her place as a world power. Because of her circumstances, therefore, America could never find any advantage in compromising her independence for the sake of any military or commercial alliance.

Sovereignty must be protected and cherished by every patriotic American. Americans, like many peoples, have always fiercely resisted efforts to take our independence by force. Our forefathers fought bravely, and against terrible odds, to win independence from the British in the Revolutionary War, and to protect it a generation later during the War of 1812. We retaliated with overwhelming force when attacked by the Japanese at Pearl Harbor in 1941. Were a foreign power somehow to launch an invasion of the United States in our time, we would surely rise up and defend our freedom and independence to the death, if need be.

But unfortunately, many Americans are not so vigilant towards attempts to deprive us of our sovereignty by *consent*.

Little by little, America has been persuaded by her enemies to surrender large chunks of her independence by entering into unwise treaties and sovereignty-sapping international organizations, like the United Nations. These modern entangling alliances not only limit our "full Power to levy War, conclude Peace, contract Alliances, establish Commerce, and to do all other Acts and Things which INDEPENDENT STATES, may of right do"; they are also completely at odds with most of our American legal, moral, and cultural traditions. Moreover, the same people and interests leading America to surrender her independence voluntarily are also working hard to encourage the cultural and political dissolution of the United States, by insisting that we tear down all international boundaries (so-called "trade barriers") and open our doors to unrestricted immigration and foreign imports.

This gradual destruction of our precious sovereignty has occurred because many Americans do not understand the nature of the enemy we now face. Instead of a brutal battlefield assault, we are facing a carefully coordinated campaign of gradual encroachment. Instead of ships and tanks, we are confronted with deceptive agreements and deliberate betrayal from within. And instead of an open, militaristic enemy regime spouting hatred and defiance, we are faced with a network of subtle conspirators prepared to use every means at their disposal to entice us into a world government. By

15

careful propaganda, by financial manipulation, and by stealthy treaties and accords, this band of powerful elitists, to be described in the next chapter, has lured America deep into a decades-old sovereignty trap.

3
The Insiders

Most of us assume that we understand how our system of government works. We learn in school about checks and balances, about the division of government into executive, legislative, and judicial branches. We learn that our government was designed in this way to safeguard against tyranny, by making sure that too much power isn't concentrated in the hands of too few people. We also know that as private citizens we may exercise certain important checks against the power of the state, such as the vote, the right to free speech, the right to keep and to bear arms, and the freedom of the press.

The Founding Fathers, for all their genius, could do no more than provide institutional and legal protections for our freedoms. They could not alter the disposition of certain men to desire power over their fellows, and they could not insulate human beings from the tendency of power, in any degree, to corrupt the human soul. Because of these human traits, freedom has always had its enemies, both at home and abroad. These enemies of freedom work tirelessly to remove and destroy the obstacles blocking them from enjoying total power. They work to undermine the Constitution, to expand and consolidate the power of the federal government, and to weaken America's cultural and moral resilience.

It has been said that the enemies of freedom never sleep. While this truth is widely appreciated, what is not widely understood is that, in our day, there exists a literal conspiracy working against the freedom of the United States and of all nations. This conspiracy exerts tremendous influence over our government, taking away our precious freedoms bit by bit in a long-term campaign of attrition. Thomas Jefferson, in the Declaration of Independence, described British tyranny in terms of "a long Train of Abuses and Usurpations, pursuing invariably the same Object" which "[evince] a Design to reduce [Americans] under absolute Despotism." Jefferson understood that when political leaders commit a long series of actions, all of which increase the power of government to oppress, we are forced to conclude that they are acting deliberately, and not merely making mistakes. In other words, when we see a "long Train of Abuses pursuing invariably the same Object," we may be sure that we are dealing with a calculated campaign to eradicate freedom. If such a campaign, and its authors, are hidden from or misrepresented to the public at large, we have a conspiracy for political power.

Many Americans are uncomfortable with the idea of political conspiracies. We sometimes like to think that cabals, revolutionary subversives, coup plotters, and the like, are found only in corrupt regimes overseas or south of the border. If our leaders make errors that enlarge the power of government, we assume that they do so because of misdirected good intentions. If they're corrupt, it's because they take bribes or get involved in extramarital affairs with interns, not because they plot for power. It's hard for many of us to believe that any of our leaders, especially those we choose at the ballot box, could be involved in anything as outrageous as a conspiracy for global control.

However, the evidence teaches us otherwise. For nearly a hundred years, a very long "train of abuses and usurpations," all of them directed at the same goal — the destruction of limited constitutional government in America, and the creation of a world government to replace it — bear sobering witness that, indeed, there exists a "design" (i.e., a conspiracy) to subject America to "absolute despotism" under a world government. We do not know what this conspiracy or its members call themselves, but we have a name for them: the Insiders.

One of our most important sources on the history of Insider activity was Georgetown University historian Carroll Quigley. In his monumental 1966 work *Tragedy and Hope,*

Quigley revealed the existence of "an international Anglophile network which operates, to some extent, in the way the radical Right believes the Communists act." He went on, with amazing candor, to describe this international secret society:

> [T]his network, which we may identify as the Round Table Groups, has no aversion to cooperating with the Communists, or any other groups, and frequently does so. I know of the operations of this network because I have studied it for twenty years and was permitted for two years, in the early 1960's, to examine its papers and secret records. I have no aversion to it or to most of its aims and have, for much of my life, been close to it and to many of its instruments. I have objected, both in the past and recently, to a few of its policies ... but in general my chief difference of opinion is that it wishes to remain unknown, and I believe its role in history is significant enough to be known.

Quigley detailed, in *Tragedy and Hope* (as well as in a second book, *The Anglo-American Establishment*), the history and objectives of what he variously referred to as the "Round Table groups" and the "Anglo-American Establishment." According to Quigley, the organization originated as a compact English secret society set up by billionaire Cecil Rhodes, with the "original purpose" of "seek[ing] to federate the English-speaking world" — that is, to consolidate the English-speaking nations of the world into a single international superstate. However, as Quigley's own work makes very clear, the true aim of this network was to create world government, not merely a super-federation of English-speaking countries. Quigley wrote extensively of the secret society's activities across the world, and of their control over the Communists:

> They ... were convinced that they could gracefully civilize the Boers of South Africa, the Irish, the Arabs, and the Hindus, and ... are largely responsible for the partitions of Ireland, Palestine, and India, as well as the federations of South Africa, Central Africa, and the West Indies. Their desire to win over the opposition by cooperation worked with Smuts but failed with Hertzog, worked with Gandhi but failed with Menon, worked with Stresemann but failed with Hitler, and has shown little chance of working with any Soviet leader.... It was this group of people, whose wealth and influence so exceeded their experience and understanding, who provided much of the framework of influence which the Communist sympathizers and fellow travelers took over in the United States in the 1930's. It must be recognized that the power these energetic Left-wingers exercised was never their own power or Communist power but was ultimately the power of the international financial coterie.

By 1915, according to Quigley, Round Table groups existed in seven countries, including "a rather loosely organized group in the United States (George Louis Beer, Walter Lippmann, Frank Aydelotte, Whitney Shepardson, Thomas W. Lamont, Jerome D. Green, Erwin D. Canham of the *Christian Science Monitor*, and others)."

The fingerprints of the Insiders first became unmistakable in the United States during and after the First World War. That conflict was the first time the United States allowed itself to be dragged into a war overseas to defend foreign interests rather than its own. President Woodrow Wilson justified the war to "make the world safe for democracy," not to defend the United States from a foreign aggressor.

But in reality, many of Wilson's decisions originated not with himself but with a mysterious individual named Edward Mandell House. "Colonel" House was a professional political operative from Texas who had also spent a lot of time in Europe and had many powerful contacts overseas. He refused all official titles from President Wilson, preferring instead to work behind the scenes. This mysterious man attracted a great deal of controversy during the Wilson administration because of his aversion to publicity. Americans rightly wanted to know what this austere Texas aristocrat was doing, unelected and unappointed, in such a position of obvious power and influence. According to Charles Seymour, compiler of House's personal papers and friend of the enigmatic Texan:

> [T]he public was mystified, especially during the early years of the Wilson administration. The circle widened that recognized in [House] a powerful factor in national and international politics, and yet few could answer the simplest questions about him. Who and what was he? Many replies were given, but, as Colonel House refused to say which were true and which false, no one was the wiser. He became the Man of Mystery…. Puzzled but untroubled, [the American public] accepted him finally as "the President's adviser." Here and there were to be heard grumbles at this strange departure in American politics; but in general, knowing little of his activities and nothing of his advice, the people came to look upon him as a wise institution.

House and Wilson were inseparable during most of Wilson's presidency; Wilson once identified House as his "second personality," claiming that "he is my independent self. His thoughts and mine are one. If I were in his place I would do just as he suggested."

And what were House's "thoughts"? In a brief span of six weeks, from late 1911 to 1912, House penned a novel, *Philip Dru: Administrator*, setting forth his agenda for

"Socialism as dreamed of by Karl Marx" in the United States of America. In the novel Philip Dru, a young West Point graduate, leads a military coup against the U.S. government. After making himself "Administrator," Dru refashions America into a fascist totalitarian dictatorship. Dru scraps the Constitution and imposes the death penalty on any who attempt to restore limited constitutional government. Dru also sets up a system of graduated income taxes and a Federal Reserve-like central banking system, and imposes a series of New Deal-like controls on labor and industry. Most interestingly for the purposes of this book, Dru also establishes an international coalition of powers similar to the League of Nations and its modern descendant, the United Nations.

Dru was influential in its day; House's associates, including Woodrow Wilson, read it with enthusiasm. But more importantly, many of its policy recommendations have been carried out, a fact that by itself testifies to House's enormous clout.

House's — and Wilson's — fondest desire was to create an international "peacemaking" body that would replace what they believed to be an outmoded international system based on alliances and conflicts among sovereign nations. Accordingly, House created "the Inquiry," a semisecret group of American elitists tasked with creating a blueprint for the international body House and his friends envisioned. The Inquiry included several of the individuals named by Quigley as members of the American Round Table group (Walter Lippmann, later to become one of America's most eminent journalists, was the group's secretary, and George Louis Beer was in charge of issues related to colonialism, to name just two examples). The Inquiry soon drafted plans for a "League of Nations" that would enforce the peace after the end of the "war to end all wars."

But events did not go the way Wilson, House, and the Inquiry intended. The League of Nations was brought into being and enthusiastically received overseas, but was ultimately rejected by the U.S. Senate. Realizing that America was not willing to accept membership in an international organization designed to trump national sovereignty, House and the rest of the Insiders decided to set up a front for their activities in the United States. Its mission would be to work, over the long term, to create conditions in the United States favorable for world government. The name of the new front organization was the Council on Foreign Relations (CFR).

The Council on Foreign Relations included House, Lippmann, Beer, Whitney Shepardson, and the other members of the original Round Table group that Carroll Quigley later identified, as well as other men of wealth and influence. Thomas W. Lamont, for example, was banker J.P. Morgan's

CEO. Dr. Isaiah Bowman, a prominent member of the Inquiry, was a Yale professor of geography who later became president of Johns Hopkins University.

The CFR made its top priority preparing the United States for entry into world government, both by molding public opinion and by insinuating its members into positions of power and influence. By the time of the Second World War, CFR members were to be found in many influential posts in the federal government, particularly in the State Department. And with the conclusion of the war, conditions were finally ripe to create an international body, a proto-world government designed along socialist lines, just as Wilson, House, and their contemporaries had dreamed of. It was primarily members of the Council on Foreign Relations who were the American architects of the United Nations system.

Since the founding of the UN system, the CFR-based "Anglo-American establishment" has grown considerably in clout. Many recent U.S. presidents, including George H. W. Bush and Bill Clinton, are or have been members of the globalist organization. CFR members have occupied and continue to occupy many of the major cabinet posts. Many of our most powerful congressmen are CFR members. So are Federal Reserve chairman Alan Greenspan and his predecessor, Paul Volcker.

The upper echelons of the mass media, Fortune 500 corporations, and the leadership of America's most prominent universities are also dominated by CFR members. Perhaps the most candid recent overview of the CFR was an article by Richard Harwood that appeared in the October 30, 1993 issue of the *Washington Post.* Calling the CFR membership "the nearest thing we have to a ruling establishment in the United States," Harwood gave a revealing summary of the CFR contingent within the Clinton administration:

> The president is a member. So is his secretary of state, the deputy secretary of state, all five of the undersecretaries, several of the assistant secretaries and the department's legal adviser. The president's national security adviser and his deputy are members. The director of Central Intelligence (like all previous directors) and the chairman of the Foreign Intelligence Advisory Board are members. The secretary of defense, three undersecretaries and at least four assistant secretaries are members. The secretaries of the departments of housing and urban development, interior, health and human services and the chief White House public relations man, David Gergen, are members, along with the speaker of the House and the majority leader of the Senate.

> This is not a retinue of people who "look like America," as

[President Clinton] once put it, but they very definitely look like the people who, for more than half a century, have managed our international affairs and our military-industrial complex.

Harwood went on to describe the influence of the CFR in the other arenas of power:

Today, two-thirds of the council's more than 2000 members live in either New York or Washington and, as you would expect, include many of the leading figures of American political life: Gerald Ford, Jimmy Carter, Henry Kissinger, Zbigniew Brzezinski, Cyrus Vance, McGeorge Bundy, Gov. Mario Cuomo and so on. Captains of industry and finance, the big universities, the big law firms and the big foundations are heavily represented.... In the past 15 years, council directors have included Hedley Donovan of Time, Inc., Elizabeth Drew of the New Yorker, Phillip Geyelin of the Washington Post, Karen Elliott House of the Wall Street Journal and Strobe Talbott of Time magazine, who is now President Clinton's ambassador at large in the Slavic world. The editorial page director, deputy editorial page director, executive editor, managing editor, foreign editor, national affairs editor, business and financial editor and various writers as well as Katherine Graham, the paper's principal owner, represent the Washington Post in the council's membership. The executive editor, managing editor and foreign editor of the New York Times are members, along with executives of such other large newspapers as the Wall Street Journal and Los Angeles Times, the weekly newsmagazines, network television executives and celebrities — Dan Rather, Tom Brokaw and Jim Lehrer, for example — and various columnists, among them Charles Krauthammer, William Buckley, George Will and Jim Hoagland.

Nothing has changed since Harwood wrote his article. CFR members dominate the administration of George W. Bush (though the president himself is not a member); prominent figures like Vice President Dick Cheney, Secretary of State Colin Powell, and National Security Advisor Condoleezza Rice are CFR members, along with dozens of others.

Nor has the agenda of the CFR changed since the organization's inception. While many of its members may not be fully aware of the CFR's true objectives, the leadership and key members are. One former prominent CFR member, Admiral Chester Ward, quit the organization after 16 years, claiming that it was "promoting disarmament and submergence of U.S. sovereignty and national independence into an all-powerful one-world government." He also noted with disgust that "this lust to surrender the sovereignty and independence of the United States is pervasive throughout most of the membership.... The majority visualize the utopian submergence of the United States as a subsidiary administrative unit of a global government."

The CFR is not the only front organization operated by the Insiders to consolidate power and to promote world government. But as the most visible, it offers convincing evidence that the building up of the United Nations system, as a prelude to world government, is taking place by design and not by accident. That most Americans fail to appreciate the influence of the CFR, despite its stunning power and prestige, is testimony of the ability of the Insiders to mask their intentions and to conceal their identity. But even though we know little about them, we see their fingerprints, from which we can infer both their existence and their agenda.

4
The UN Sovereignty Trap

E ntomologists — people who collect and study insects — have various methods of luring and trapping the creatures they study. One of the most effective is called the "sugar trap." A sugar trap isn't hard to make. A can or bucket is filled with water, to which is added sugar and various kinds of fruits. The concoction is then hung from a tree in a place where lots of insects are likely to pass. As anyone who has picnicked outdoors knows, many types of insects are attracted to sweet-tasting foods.

The interesting property of the sugar trap is that it becomes more and more effective the longer it stays in place. At first, the sugar water will attract only a few moths and flies that will gather almost anywhere. But after a few days, the fruit in the concoction starts to ferment and the smell becomes stronger and sweeter. When this occurs, the trap becomes a magnet for many kinds of insects, attracted from far and wide by the powerful aroma. All of them are drawn to the sweet concoction, but as soon as they land in the sugar trap to feed, they are caught in the sticky liquid and drown. A sugar trap left outside for a couple of weeks will often snare hundreds of insects.

The United Nations system is designed to function something like a sugar trap. Its creators — the Insiders — knew they could not create instant world government. So they designed instead an organization whose framework would allow it to be strengthened over time. Like the contents of the sugar trap, the longer the United Nations survives, the more rotten the system becomes, and the greater its power.

John Foster Dulles, a founding member of the CFR and early supporter of the United Nations who later became President Eisenhower's secretary of state, explained the potential of the United Nations in his book *War or Peace*:

> I have never seen any proposal made for collective security with "teeth" in it, or for "world government" or for "world federation," which could not be carried out either by the United Nations or under the United Nations Charter.
>
> If the principal members of the United Nations, including the Soviet Union, are willing to take part in a proposed new world organization, then the United Nations itself could quickly be made into that organization.

Why would Dulles believe this? In the first place, we must understand, as Dulles did, that the United Nations is a governmental, not a private, organization. Therefore, all UN functions, principles, and goals are *government* projects. When the UN Charter (the "constitution" of the United Nations) tells us, for example (as it does, in Chapter 1, Article 1), that the purposes of the United Nations include "tak[ing] effective collective measures for the prevention and removal of threats to the peace" and "achiev[ing] international cooperation in solving international problems of an economic, social, cultural, or humanitarian character," it is proposing *governmental* solutions to such problems.

And that's a big part of the problem. The United Nations Charter is based not on the principles of freedom and limited government but on *socialism*, which assumes that all human problems must be solved by the power of government planning, disguised as "collective action." Socialism in all its forms — including communism — is dangerous to the liberty and well-being of any people, and is also completely at odds with the limited powers granted to our federal government by the Constitution. A socialist government by definition has no limits on its power, because socialism requires the state to spend any amount of money, hire any number of officials, pass any needed laws, and give itself any needed amount of police and military power to enforce its will on a captive citizenry. Once the socialist creed is adopted, state power will mushroom, and may eventually spawn horrors

33

like German Nazism (the very term "Nazism," incidentally, is short for "National Socialism"). Socialism, therefore, has no place in the United States of America. We cannot have both socialism and freedom.

A very large component of the United Nations has always been dedicated to international socialism in the form of state-sponsored welfare projects. Chapter 9, Article 55 of the UN Charter stipulates that the UN "shall promote ... higher standards of living, full employment, and conditions of economic and social progress and development [and] solutions of international economic, social, health, and related problems; and international cultural and educational cooperation." The United Nations includes many subsidiary international organizations responsible for activities ranging from the welfare of the world's children (UNICEF) and health (WHO) to education, science and culture (UNESCO). State-sponsored activity in all of these areas is the very essence of socialism, and, as we have seen, is at variance with the American tradition of limited, constitutional government. For this reason alone, Americans cannot uphold both the UN Charter and the U.S. Constitution. And as long as our nation belongs to the United Nations, our system of limited government will be under constant pressure to conform to the UN's ambitious social engineering goals.

The most powerful body in the United Nations is the

Security Council. It consists of 15 members of the United Nations, of whom five — the United States, China, France, Russia, and Great Britain — are permanent members, while the other 10 are elected by UN member states for two-year terms. The UN Charter clothes the Security Council with both legislative and executive authority. The Council has the power to deliberate and to issue resolutions, which, from the point of view of the United Nations, have the force of law and must be observed by all UN member states. If any offending nation disregards such resolutions, the Security Council then has the authority to use all measures, including unlimited war, to enforce the will of the United Nations. Articles 41 and 42 of the Charter spell these powers out very plainly:

> The Security Council may decide what measures not involving the use of armed force are to be employed to give effect to its decisions, and it may call upon the Members of the United Nations to apply such measures. These may include complete or partial interruption of economic relations and of rail, sea, air, postal, telegraphic, radio, and other means of communication, and the severance of diplomatic relations.
>
> Should the Security Council consider that [such] measures … would be inadequate or have proved to be inadequate, it may take such action by air, sea, or land forces as may be necessary to maintain or restore international peace and security.

Such action may include demonstrations, blockade, and
other operations by air, sea, or land forces of Members of the
United Nations.

The Security Council, in other words, has — according to
the UN Charter — final authority over all international disputes as well as any domestic problems that it decides are
"threats to the peace," "breaches of the peace," or "acts of
aggression." And to enforce its will, the Security Council has
the power to make war in order to prevent war — a very curi-
ous provision for an organization supposedly charged with
keeping the peace!

The Security Council is empowered not only to wage war
against aggressors, but also, in conjunction with the rest of
the UN organization, to dictate to member states the course
of peaceful relations among them. The Council, by the terms
of Chapter 8 of the UN Charter, has final authority over all
regional security arrangements, such as NATO. The United
Nations as a whole also has ultimate authority over all treaties
entered into by member states; Articles 102 and 103 of
Chapter 16 of the UN Charter stipulate that "every treaty and
every international agreement entered into by any Member of
the United Nations after the present Charter comes into force
shall as soon as possible be registered with the Secretariat and
published with it…. In the event of a conflict between the

obligations of the Members of the United Nations under the present Charter and their obligations under any other international agreement, their obligations under the present Charter shall prevail."

The Security Council is also the seat of final appeal for judgments rendered by the UN's International Court of Justice (more commonly known as the World Court), according to Chapter 14 of the Charter:

> Each Member of the United Nations undertakes to comply with the decision of the International Court of Justice in any case to which it is a party.
>
> If any party to a case fails to perform the obligations incumbent upon it under a judgment rendered by the Court, the other party may have recourse to the Security Council, which may, if it deems necessary, make recommendations or decide upon measures to be taken to give effect to the judgment.

The Security Council has a terrifying array of powers, on paper at least: the power to wage unlimited war; the power to impose total trade embargos and sanctions; and the power to act as a court of last appeal regarding disputes between member states. But even more importantly, it has the power to define offenses and to set rules arbitrarily. It is to become, very literally, an international judge, jury, and executioner, where the conduct of member states is concerned. As John Foster Dulles bluntly put it:

> The Security Council is not a body that merely enforces agreed law. It is a law unto itself. If it considers any situation as a threat to the peace, it may decide what measures shall be taken. No principles of law are laid down to guide it; it can decide in accordance with what it thinks is expedient.

The UN Charter was also designed to permit the United Nations as a whole to accumulate powers far beyond those mentioned explicitly, as Dulles clearly understood. In addition to the unlimited grant of power to the Security Council, the Charter also grants the United Nations unlimited legal authority — that is, absolute power — wherever and however it chooses to carry out its objectives. Thus, according to the deceptively bland language in Chapter 16, Article 104, "The Organization shall enjoy in the territory of each of its Members such legal capacity as may be necessary for the exercise of its functions and the fulfillment of its purposes."

Imagine now what America would be like if the United Nations discharged all of the functions and took full advantage of all the authorities granted in its charter. First of all, our federal government would need to seek the United Nations' approval for all treaties entered into. It would not be able to wage war without the UN's permission. The federal government would be forced to send American fighting men anywhere in the world that the Security Council decided to exercise its war powers. In the event of any domestic disturbances or quarrels, such as urban rioting, the United States might be required by the Security Council to permit UN troops to keep the peace. If another country registered a complaint to the Security Council against the United States, the Council might rule against the United States and compel us to meet the terms of a hostile regime.

Furthermore, the U.S. government would also be forced to bring its laws into conformity with the UN's socialist agenda to guarantee socialist "rights" like full employment and state-controlled health services. To whatever degree the United Nations deemed proper, American wealth would be taken from taxpayers and redistributed to the governments of poorer nations.

Given the language of the UN Charter and the makeup of the UN organization, none of this is far-fetched. It is in fact a comparatively benign scenario of life in a world where national sovereignty has been replaced by socialist world government under the United Nations. But the most appalling aspect of this scenario is that *most of it has already come to pass!* American troops are already deployed all over the world under United Nations authority, from the former Yugoslavia to South Korea. Recent American military actions in Iraq, Haiti, and Somalia were also carried out under UN authority. The U.S. government routinely seeks UN authorization before going to war. The first President Bush sought, and obtained, UN authorization to wage war against Iraq following Saddam Hussein's invasion of Kuwait, and his son did the same before launching the War on Terrorism in Afghanistan. Moreover, U.S. arms control treaties, such as the Bush-Putin accord to reduce nuclear arsenals, are routinely registered with the United Nations.

The United States is under constant international pressure to change its laws to comply with UN-sponsored global agreements promoting international socialism in various forms. In spring of 2002, for example, the Bush administration signed the Monterrey Protocol, which contains language effectively calling for global taxation and for nations to "harmonize" their tax laws to agree with UN standards. President Bush has also indicated a willingness to change U.S. environmental laws to comply with the spirit, if not the letter, of the Kyoto Accord, a UN-brokered treaty that would impose global emissions standards and other international environmental regulations on American industries. And for several decades, billions of taxpayer dollars have been sent overseas in the form of government foreign aid, much of it administered by the UN-affiliated World Bank and the IMF.

The major difference between our hypothetical scenario and current reality is that the United Nations cannot yet *compel* the United States to do anything. We remain both militarily and economically strong enough to resist any UN attempts to force us to heel. Yet many of the UN's most dangerous objectives are being accomplished, because the U.S. government, under the influence of the pro-UN internationalist Insiders, voluntarily defers to UN authority whenever it can.

In other words, we are losing our sovereignty to the United Nations by consent — the consent of pro-UN politicians in Washington motivated by the desire to deliver the United States into world government under the UN system by every unsavory, underhanded trick they can devise. If we continue down this path, we will soon find ourselves permanently ensnared in the UN system. Instead of a consensual relationship, the UN will compel the United States to meet its terms, by economic and military force if necessary — as it already has the power to do with most other nations in the world.

The UN sugar trap has already claimed many victims, and its power has grown enormously since its founding. From the original 50 member states, membership in the UN is now almost universal. The UN has burgeoned in influence from a "debating society" to an embryonic world government. The UN now has the power to crush by force powerful dictatorial regimes like Saddam Hussein's Iraq and Slobodan Milosevic's Yugoslavia — a seeming benefit, until we remember that the UN and its Insider sponsors fully intend to amass similar power over *all* governments, good and bad, including, eventually, our own. The UN also oversees the redistribution of billions of taxpayer dollars worldwide. It exerts growing influence in the United States over foreign policy and even over domestic lawmaking. In size, power, and prestige, the United Nations is now very close to what its creators hoped it would become. In the following chapters, we will take a closer look at just how far the United Nations has come, in just a few areas of concern, towards functioning in the way its founders intended.

5
Wars and Rumors of Wars

There's nothing new about war. Nations, tribes, and kingdoms have resorted to war for a variety of reasons since the beginning of recorded history. By the time of America's Founding Fathers civilized nations had started to think about alternatives to all-out warfare. After all, recent centuries had witnessed the Hundred Years' War between France and England, the Thirty Years' War involving most of the powers on the European continent, the bloody English civil war of the mid-17th century, and devastating religious wars, to name only a few. Building on the ideas of early Christian thinkers like St. Augustine, men such as Hugo Grotius, a 17th-century Dutch political philosopher, and Emmerich de Vattel, an 18th-century Swiss jurist, wrote books describing the principles of "just war." They believed that, in order to be justified, war ought to be used only as a last resort, should normally be defensive, not offensive, and should avoid deliberate attacks on civilian populations. To wage total war for plunder, profit, or conquest was the mark of the barbarian.

Under the influence of such ideas, the American Founders determined that the best way to avoid war was to be as neutral as possible concerning the quarrels and affairs of other nations. They adopted this principle of neutrality as their national policy. George Washington, in his Farewell Address, advised Americans:

> The great rule of conduct for us, in regard to foreign nations is, in extending our commercial relations, to have with them as little political connection as possible.... Europe has a set of primary interests, which to us have none, or a very remote relation. Hence she must be engaged in frequent controversies, the causes of which are essentially foreign to our concerns.... It is our true policy to steer clear of permanent alliance with any portion of the foreign world.

Thomas Jefferson later echoed this sentiment, in a letter to President James Monroe:

> Our first and fundamental maxim should be, never to entangle ourselves in the broils of Europe; our second, never to suffer Europe to intermeddle with [trans]-Atlantic affairs.

And John Quincy Adams said:

[America] goes not abroad in search of monsters to destroy. She is the well-wisher to the freedom and independence of all. She is the champion and vindicator only of her
own.... She well knows that by once enlisting under other
banners than her own, were they even the banners of foreign
independence, she would involve herself beyond the power
of extrication in all wars of interest and intrigue, envy and
ambition, which assume the colors and usurp the standards
of freedom.

All of these statements amount to a very simple principle, as sound in international affairs as it is in interper-
sonal conduct: Mind your own business.

Such a foreign policy is wise for several reasons. One
is that we cannot expect to understand all of the complex-
ities of quarrels among foreign nations. Many conflicts
have roots reaching back for centuries and involve cultural,
religious, or linguistic differences that we cannot possibly
appreciate fully. Another is the principle, explained earlier,
that all sovereign nations deserve to be treated with equal
respect, as long as they do not provoke us directly. To take
sides in any conflict involving third-party nations is to
show unjustified favoritism.

Yet another reason for a policy of non-interventionism
is the cost of war. Any war involves terrible sacrifice, both

of wealth and human life. The Founders believed that Americans should not be asked to supply money and lives in defense of foreign nations, and that only self-defense could possibly justify the terrible price of war.

The Constitution divides war powers between the legislative and executive branches of the federal government. Congress is given the power to raise revenue for military forces and to declare war, while the president is empowered to be the commander-in-chief of all United States military forces. The president is not, however, permitted to dispatch troops anywhere he pleases, or to engage in sustained acts of war without a congressional declaration of war.

The Founders made it clear that they did not intend to give the president the war powers enjoyed by the British monarch. As Alexander Hamilton explained, in *The Federalist*, No. 69:

> The President is to be commander-in-chief of the army and navy of the United States. In this respect his authority would be nominally the same with that of the king of Great Britain, but in substance much inferior to it. It would amount to nothing more than the supreme command and direction of the military and naval forces, as first general and admiral of the confederacy; while that of the British king extends to

the declaring of war and to the raising and regulating of fleets and armies — all which, by the Constitution under consideration, would appertain to the legislature.

Yet for almost a century, the Insiders have been maneuvering America into one foreign conflict after another, from World War I to the present-day global "war on terrorism." With the exception of World Wars I and II, none of these wars has been initiated by a congressional declaration of war, and every one since 1945 has therefore been in violation of constitutional war powers. None of these modern wars has been a defensive action against a full-fledged invading power, and only two (World War II and the Afghanistan phase of the War on Terrorism) have even been in response to an attack on the United States. Sadly, many of our modern wars have involved systematic campaigns of terror against civilians and military personnel alike, from the atomic incineration of Hiroshima and Nagasaki to the deliberate bombing of civilian targets in Iraq and Serbia.

For the United States, modern warfare since World War II has been almost exclusively a by-product of our relationship with the UN. In 1945, at the time the United Nations was coming into being, one astute statesman, J. Reuben Clark, former undersecretary of state and U.S.

ambassador to Mexico, foresaw the consequences of creating an organization to wage collective war in the name of peace. He wrote, regarding the UN Charter, that "the Charter is a war document not a peace document.... [It] makes us a party to every international dispute arising anywhere in the world." Clark also predicted that the United Nations would "not prevent future wars, [and make] it practically certain that we shall have future wars, and as to such wars it takes from us the power to declare them, to choose the side on which we shall fight, to determine what forces and military equipment we shall use in the war, and to control and command our sons who do the fighting."

In 1950, President Harry S. Truman sent U.S. troops to fight under UN rules in what became the Korean War, a bloody, three-year conflict that displayed for the first time the UN's power to wage war in the name of peace. The Korean War, which cost more than 36,000 American lives, was the first time that America went to war without a constitutionally required congressional declaration. When Congress attempted to stop Truman from committing American forces to Korea without a declaration of war, he replied that the Korean conflict was not a war but a "police action" authorized by the UN Charter. In other words, Truman believed that our new obligations to the United Nations overruled the U.S. Constitution.

The Korean War ended in a UN-brokered stalemate. The agreement that terminated open hostilities created what UN insiders call a "ceasefire." A ceasefire, it is important to understand, is very different from a "peace treaty." A peace treaty is an agreement by which two hostile powers come to terms and officially end the state of war existing between them. The United States signed peace treaties with both Japan and Germany at the end of World War II, and in the years that followed America has enjoyed friendly diplomatic and trade relations with both countries.

On the other hand, a "ceasefire" (or truce) does not end a state of war, but only terminates open conflict. According to the terms of a ceasefire, both hostile powers agree to suspend open hostilities in order to negotiate, but a state of war continues. Ceasefires can and often do break down, until one side forces the other to surrender and sign a peace treaty. In stark contrast to the situation with Germany and Japan, North and South Korea remain technically at war 50 years after the "end" of the Korean War. Thousands of American and South Korean troops patrol the DMZ, or Demilitarized Zone, separating the two Koreas, while North Korea's million-man army waits on hair-trigger alert to launch a new invasion of the hated South. The Communist North Korean government, one of the world's most repressive regimes, frequently sends terrorists and assassins to attack military and civilian targets in South Korea. With the help of the Communist Chinese, the North Koreans have developed sophisticated guided missile technology, and may now have the means to attack American territory with long-range missiles. It is also probable that North Korea has acquired nuclear weapons. Such is the nature of "peace," United Nations-style.

The Korean War established many terrible precedents that have been observed ever since. Constitutional war powers have been ignored as American presidents have dragged America into one conflict after another without a congressional declaration of war. American leaders have required U.S. servicemen to fight under the UN banner, and sometimes even to wear the distinctive blue helmets identifying UN military forces. American troops have also been compelled by their own leaders to serve under foreign commanders representing the United Nations.

The world has changed a lot in the half century since the Korean War, and some of us might assume that the United Nations has as well. But during that time, the UN has become the world's premier agent for war, not peace, and always follows the same pattern in responding to a crisis: The Security Council, having ascertained a threat to "international peace" or "stability," dispatches military forces to the "trouble spot," which then coerce the warring parties to come to terms, in the process waging pitiless war against the guilty and innocent alike.

In 1960, the former Belgian Congo became independent from Belgium. Within days of independence Soviet Communist surrogate Patrice Lumumba, who had been made premier of the new nation, unleashed a reign of terror against the Congolese. His actions prompted the province of Katanga, led by the Christian, pro-Western Moise Tshombe, to secede from the Congo. For a few months, an independent and free Katanga was an island of calm and relative prosperity. But the pro-Communist Insiders at the UN and in the U.S. government had other plans for Katanga. Clearly, an independent, stable regime in the heart of Africa posed an unacceptable challenge to the Insiders' plans for hegemony over that continent.

In July of 1960, following a UN resolution authorizing the use of UN forces in the Congo, and jointly supported by the United States and the USSR, thousands of UN troops were dispatched to the region. After three brutal military campaigns spanning three and a half years, in which UN forces ravaged Katanga, indiscriminately massacring thousands of civilians including many European residents, free Katanga was vanquished and Moise Tshombe exiled to Europe. Though Tshombe later returned briefly as premier of the entire Congo under President Kasavubu, the unhappy

African nation never recovered from the events associated with the attempted Katangan secession. Today, following several decades of horrific oppression under the heel of UN-approved dictator Mobutu Sese Seko, the impoverished region has once again descended into chaos and civil war. The United Nations, meanwhile, oversees much of Africa; its largest current "peacekeeping" project is in the hapless West African nation of Sierra Leone, where thousands of UN troops protect rival factions from each other — while safeguarding that country's fabulous diamond mining operations.

But the UN hasn't confined its military activities to obscure African countries. In August 1990, Iraqi dictator Saddam Hussein's forces stormed into the oil-rich Persian Gulf state of Kuwait. Within days, the first President Bush resolved to "liberate" Kuwait, by military force if necessary. Once again, it appeared, the United States was going to send military forces overseas to wage war against a country that posed no threat to the United States and that, until recently, had enjoyed U.S. support in its war against Iran.

But President Bush did not seek a congressional declaration of war. He made it plain to Congress that he expected a rubber stamp for what he was about to do, and that he would wage war on Iraq no matter what Congress wanted. Within days after the Iraqi invasion, President Bush sent U.S. troops to Saudi Arabia. In a brief letter to congres-

George Washington:

"The great rule of conduct for us, in regard to foreign nations is, in extending our commercial relations, to have with them as little political connection as possible."

Museum of the City of New York/Corbis

Thomas Jefferson:

"Our first and fundamental maxim should be, never to entangle ourselves in the broils of Europe."

Burstein Collection/Corbis

The Corcoran Gallery/Corbis

John Quincy Adams:

"[America] goes not abroad in search of monsters to destroy. She is the well-wisher to the freedom and independence of all. She is the champion and vindicator only of her own."

Declaration of Independence:

"These United Colonies are, and of a Right ought to be, FREE AND INDEPENDENT STATES ... and that as FREE and INDEPENDENT STATES, they have full Power to levy War, conclude Peace, contract Alliances, establish Commerce, and do all other Acts and Things which INDEPENDENT STATES, may of right do."

Courtesy National Archives

James Madison:

"The freemen of America did not wait till usurped power had strengthened itself by exercise and entangled the question in precedents. They saw all the consequences in principle, and they avoided the consequences by denying the principle."

Below: *Conferees at Dumbarton Oaks, August 21, 1944.*
Inset: *U.S. Secretary of State Edward Stettinius signs the UN treaty in San Francisco, June 1945, while President Truman (far left) looks on.*

Above: *The Bretton Woods conference, July 1, 1944.*
Below: *Mt. Washington hotel at Bretton Woods, New Hampshire.*

Above: *Carroll Quigley*
Below: *Headquarters of the International Monetary Fund, Washington, D.C.*

Above: *UN Secretary-General Kofi Annan at Columbia University.*
Below: *Pratt House in New York City, where the Council on Foreign Relations is headquartered.*

J. Reuben Clark:
"The [UN] Charter is a war document not a peace document."
Above Right: *The League of Nations in its opening session, November 1920*
Below: *President Woodrow Wilson (left) and Mrs. Wilson, with "Colonel" Edward Mandell House.*

FREEDOM
FROM
WAR

THE UNITED STATES PROGRAM FOR GENERAL AND COMPLETE DISARMAMENT IN A PEACEFUL WORLD

Above: *UN armed forces on patrol in Sierra Leone, West Africa.*

Freedom From War: *"No state would have the military power to challenge the progressively strengthened U.N. Peace Force."*

Below: *U.S. troops under NATO and UN authority in Kosovo conduct a house-to-house search for weapons, accompanied by United Nations police officials.*

sional leaders, Bush offered as justification, in the very first sentence, the fact that "Iraq invaded and occupied the sovereign state of Kuwait in flagrant violation of the Charter of the United Nations." Once again, the United States was preparing to do the UN's bidding.

Over the next several months, the United Nations issued resolutions condemning Iraq's action and supported President Bush in assembling a vast, multinational coalition of military forces. Besides the United States, France, Great Britain, Germany, Italy, Saudi Arabia, and even countries as far-removed as Argentina contributed planes, ships, and personnel to the UN coalition.

On January 16, 1991, the United Nations coalition launched a massive saturation bombing campaign in Iraq, attacking military and civilian targets all over the country. President Bush addressed the American people two hours after the war started. "This military action," he announced, "taken in accord with United Nations resolutions and with the consent of the United States Congress, follows months of constant and virtually endless diplomatic activity on the part of the United Nations." Leaving no doubt who was in charge of the operation, Bush assured Americans that "Iraq will eventually comply with all relevant United Nations resolutions, and then, when peace is restored, ... will live as a peaceful and cooperative member of the family of nations.... The United States, together with the United Nations, exhausted every means at our disposal to bring this crisis to a peaceful end. However, Saddam clearly felt that by stalling and threatening and defying the United Nations, he could weaken the forces arrayed against him .... Saddam was warned over and over to comply with the will of the United Nations: leave Kuwait, or be driven out." Finally, President Bush outlined his vision of the future that the Gulf War would usher in:

> This is an historic moment.... We have before us the opportunity to forge for ourselves and for future generations a new world order — a world where the rule of law, not the law of the jungle, governs the conduct of nations. When we are successful — and we will be — we have a real chance at this new world order, an order in which a credible United Nations can use its peacekeeping role to fulfill the vision and promise of the UN's founders.

In the war that followed, stealth bombers, cruise missiles, and other terrifying modern superweapons killed thousands of Iraqi civilians and terrorized the rest. After weeks of nonstop bombing, the UN coalition launched a huge land invasion of Iraq. As coalition forces raced north, a quick victory seemed assured. Many observers assumed that UN coalition forces would enter Baghdad, topple Saddam Hussein, and force Iraq to surrender.

But that is not what happened. To the frustration of many Americans, who expected, after the fiascos in Korea and Vietnam, that this time we would finish the job, President Bush suddenly and inexplicably called off the offensive. United Nations negotiators then stepped in and negotiated, not a surrender but a ceasefire. Under the terms of the ceasefire, Saddam Hussein remained in power with substantial portions of his military intact. He was required to submit to a permanent regime of UN "weapons inspectors," who were to be given unlimited access to Iraqi facilities as they searched for chemical, biological, and possibly nuclear weapons and research facilities to destroy. UN forces, including a generous number of American planes and pilots, began to patrol "no-fly zones" in northern and southern Iraq.

The purpose of the no-fly zones was ostensibly to prevent Saddam Hussein from threatening his neighbors or U.S. bases with the remnants of his air power. But these zones did not prevent Saddam Hussein from launching retaliatory campaigns against the Kurds in the north and the Shiites in the south, who had risen against him in the belief that the coalition forces would help them overthrow their odious dictator. UN and U.S. forces, however, stood by passively and let Saddam Hussein brutally crush both rebellions, slaughtering thousands more and further strengthening his grip on the helpless Iraqi people.

President Bush regarded the Gulf War as an unqualified success. In a televised address to Congress on March 6th, he proclaimed:

> Now, we can see a new world coming into view. A world in which there is the very real prospect of a new world order.... A world where the United Nations, freed from cold war stalemate, is poised to fulfill the historic vision of its founders.

The Gulf War, however, was not over. It merely went dormant, with U.S. and other coalition forces on permanent patrol over the skies of Iraq, attacking Iraqi facilities such as anti-aircraft batteries almost weekly. Meanwhile, Saddam Hussein played a canny shell game with UN inspectors on the ground. The inspectors were permitted to locate and destroy some Iraqi weapons, but many more were moved from place to place, while Saddam Hussein quietly began rebuilding his military. UN trade sanctions strangled the Iraqi economy, leading to impoverishment and deteriorating health standards across Iraq. Thousands more Iraqis died as a result of malnutrition and disease.

In June 1993, the cold Gulf War heated up again when President Clinton launched a cruise missile assault against Baghdad in retaliation for an Iraqi plot to assassinate ex-President Bush. In the summer of 1998, an emboldened Saddam Hussein expelled the UN weapons inspectors from Iraq. The war flared up for a third time a few months later, in December 1998, when an embattled President Clinton, in an attempt to stave off impeachment, launched another heavy air campaign against Iraq, Operation Desert Fox, that lasted four days. The attack had only limited effect, and over the next several years Saddam Hussein has continued to re-build his military.

Shortly after taking office, President George W. Bush launched yet another series of fierce air strikes against Iraq. And so it stands. At the time of this writing, more than a decade after the Gulf War, Saddam Hussein is still in power, U.S. and coalition forces still patrol the skies of Iraq, and the UN trade embargo remains intact. As should now be obvious, neither the UN nor the first President Bush ever had the slightest intention of ousting Saddam Hussein or of prosecuting a clear-cut military victory (and should Saddam Hussein ever be ousted, his successor will no doubt be another UN-approved puppet). Instead, we settled for yet another "ceasefire" to protect a brutal regime and keep it in its box, while giving the UN legitimacy. The real purpose of the Gulf War and its aftermath, as President Bush stated openly on more than one occasion, was to lay the foundation for a "new world order" in which the United Nations would finally be able to live up to the bellicose potential its founders had envisioned.

Just as it had done in Katanga three decades earlier, the UN demonstrated with the Gulf War the real nature of its "peacekeeping mission." As a result of UN interference in the Persian Gulf, a local conflict between two hostile neighbors was turned into a global war, with the armed forces of 28 UN member states drawn into the conflict. And a war that had been comparatively bloodless was turned into a monstrous bloodbath in which as many as 100,000 Iraqis and more than 140 American troops were killed and large sections of Iraqi cities bombed into powder. Moreover, thanks to the United Nations, a relatively inconsequential act of local aggression that was over within hours (Iraq's original invasion and conquest of Kuwait) was transformed into a permanent state of war with intermittent new bombing campaigns and a convenient excuse to establish a huge, permanent U.S. military presence in the volatile Middle East. And through it all, Saddam Hussein, one of the world's most brutal dictators, remains in power, outlasting two U.S. presidents, two British prime ministers, and numerous other world leaders who were involved at one time or another in the campaign to contain him. This has been the cost of going "abroad in search of monsters to destroy" under UN authority.

Toward the end of the first George Bush's presidency, the major news media began publishing heart-wrenching coverage of the civil war and famine unfolding in the east African country of Somalia. Photos of starving children with bloated bellies and fly-covered faces soon prompted calls for international intervention in Somalia. In the last days of his presidency, having already lost the election to Bill Clinton, George Bush sought and obtained UN authorization to launch an invasion of Somalia in conjunction with multinational UN forces, supposedly to supply humanitarian aid and to restore peace to the troubled region.

At first everything went well. The operation resembled a media event more than a war, as American Marines landed on the Somali beaches under the glare of television klieg lights. The entire operation seemed to be a risk-free tune-up, and the local Somalis appeared to welcome the international force.

But before long, the United Nations began carrying out arrests and attacks against local warlords and their factions. American forces participated in UN-mandated hit-and-run missions in Mogadishu, the Somali capital. On one occasion, in July of 1993, U.S. helicopter gunships attacked a large group of unarmed Somalis meeting in a house in Mogadishu, killing more than 50.

One Somali warlord in particular, Mohammed Farah Aidid, was branded the chief instigator of the violence in Mogadishu after his forces attacked a contingent of Pakistani peacekeeping troops. The UN began searching for the elusive Aidid, conducting perodic raids. On October 3, 1993, the United States launched a raid on a Mogadishu hotel where Aidid was believed to be holed up, intending to swoop in and spirit him away into UN detention. But things went badly wrong. As American elite forces converged on their target, Aidid's militiamen opened fire, downing two Black Hawk helicopters and trapping a large number of U.S. soldiers in the heart of hostile Mogadishu. A fierce battle erupted as the well-armed American soldiers tried to fight their way out of the city. Aidid's forces sniped away from buildings and alleyways, eventually killing 18 U.S. servicemen, taking one hostage, and wounding dozens more. Meanwhile, the American forces killed hundreds, perhaps thousands, of Somalis on that terrible day, many of them civilians in Mogadishu's crowded marketplace.

At the end of the day, U.S. troops retreated in defeat. Mohammed Farah Aidid remained at large, and the American news broadcast horrifying images of furious Somali crowds dragging the body of a dead U.S. serviceman through the streets of Mogadishu.

UN and U.S. forces eventually left Somalia, their mission a complete failure. Once again, thousands of lives, including those of a number of Americans, had been snuffed out in the name of UN "peacekeeping." Today, Somalia continues to suffer from intermittent clan warfare and is a major haven for international terrorism, including Osama bin Laden's al-Qaeda.

If Iraq and Somalia were George Bush's contributions to international, UN-supervised peacekeeping, then Bill Clinton will surely be remembered for involving the United States in the Balkan quagmire. Communist Yugoslavia had originally been cobbled together by dictator Josip Broz Tito, who united under a single banner peoples professing three religions and speaking four different major languages. After the lifting of the Iron Curtain, Yugoslavia began to disintegrate, despite the efforts of Communist dictator Slobodan Milosevic to hold the country together. The secession of Bosnia and Croatia ignited a fierce three-sided civil war among the Serbs, the Croats, and the Bosnian Muslims. The better-trained and more heavily armed Serbian regulars inflicted defeat after defeat on both Croat and Bosnian forces. Well-publicized sieges of Sarajevo and Srebrenica generated outrage in the press, with the inevitable calls for "the international community" to "do something." President Bush had avoided getting the U.S. involved in the former Yugoslavia, but President Clinton, eager to play the peacemaker, plunged in. U.S. forces under NATO command were soon attacking Serb positions in Bosnia (NATO, it is not widely known, has always been a UN "regional arrangement" under articles 52-54 of the UN Charter).

The rationale for this latest military adventure was familiar enough: The Balkan conflict threatened to "destabilize" Europe. Before long, NATO/UN troops, including American soldiers placed under UN command, were patrolling Bosnia and Croatia.

But the fighting continued. UN troops looked on as Serb forces continued to inflict defeats on Bosnian Muslims. In 1995, Croatia, whom Serbia had defeated in the first go-round, launched a retaliatory campaign against the Serbs. Better armed than before, the Croats drove the Serbs out of large portions of conquered territory.

No sooner had Bosnia and Croatia settled down than the Serbian-controlled region of Kosovo erupted. Kosovo was the traditional heartland of Serbian culture and history, but in recent decades a massive influx of Albanian immigrants had changed the ethnic balance. Now, the Muslim Albanians launched a war of secession against the

Serbs, fully expecting the United Nations and NATO forces to support them.

Nor were they disappointed. When the Serbs launched a military operation against Kosovo, the Western press began reporting unsubstantiated accounts of Serbian atrocities — detention camps, massacres, and mass graves — committed against the Albanians. The Albanians were oppressed freedom fighters, went the official line, and must be helped against their Serb oppressors.

The truth of the matter was completely at odds with official propaganda. The Albanian "freedom fighters" — the KLA (Kosovo Liberation Army) — were in fact a band of terrorists, drug runners, and ruffians with known ties to international terrorism and drug trafficking in the United States.

Nevertheless, Insiders at NATO and the UN, determined to take control of Kosovo, plunged ahead. President Clinton, only recently acquitted by the U.S. Senate at his impeachment trial, embarked on a brutal air war against Serbia in early 1999, to force the Serbs out of Kosovo. Civilian targets in Serbia were bombed alongside Serbian positions in Kosovo. U.S. and NATO warplanes attacked electricity and news facilities, claiming roughly 2,000 Serbian lives, many of them civilians. Once again, internationalist Insiders had managed to transform a tiny regional conflict into an international war.

As with Croatia and Bosnia, UN, NATO, and U.S. forces soon occupied Kosovo and began keeping the peace, with the postwar peacekeeping mission under UN command. By the end of the 1990s, UN forces occupied almost all of the former Yugoslavia. Only Slovenia had seceded peacefully; the remainder of the region, including tiny Macedonia, was now a de facto UN trust territory, and there is no indication that the UN ever intends to give up its prize. Since the American military is the backbone of UN forces in the Balkans, our troops are likely to remain trapped in the Balkan quagmire, with its tinderbox politics, for a very long time.

On September 11, 2001, civilian jetliners piloted by terrorist hijackers hurtled out of the clear blue sky into the twin towers of the World Trade Center in lower Manhattan and the Pentagon outside Washington, D.C. A fourth hijacked jet plane crashed in a field near Shanksville in western Pennsylvania, apparently en route to another target in Washington. As Americans watched in horror on live TV, first one and then the other World Trade Center towers collapsed into flaming ruins, killing thousands of people and engulfing lower Manhattan in a massive cloud of smoke, dust and debris. Within a few days, Bush administration officials announced that the al-Qaeda terrorist network of Osama bin Laden was likely responsible for the catastrophic attack. Because al-Qaeda was known to have its headquarters in Afghanistan, sheltered and supported by the fundamentalist Muslim Taliban regime, the United States began preparing for yet another overseas military campaign, the first major operation in what has become known as the "War on Terrorism."

President George W. Bush, following the now-familiar pattern, informed the UN Security Council of his intentions and sought the Council's approval. The Security Council gave President Bush its full support, and on September 28 issued resolution 1373, a new set of rules for member states to follow in order to combat terrorism.

Resolution 1373 represents a new phase in the empowerment of the United Nations over member states. It requires member states to bring their laws into compliance with new UN-mandated anti-terrorism standards, which include stringent state controls on financial transactions and arms sales and possession, as well as enhanced government powers of surveillance.

Resolution 1373 also created a new UN Counter-Terrorism Committee (CTC) under the Security Council, whose mission is to make sure member states comply with the UN's new counter-terrorism standards. Under the new UN counter-terrorism regime, member states report to the CTC their progress in changing their laws to conform with the requirements of Resolution 1373. The CTC in turn issues regular directives to member states, outlining further legal reforms they must make.

The U.S. government has been cooperating with the Counter-Terrorism Committee and submitting the required "progress reports." The CTC in turn has been exerting pressure on the U.S. to strengthen national firearms laws and financial disclosure laws, among other things. As the CTC's own documents make clear, this new process of CTC browbeating is intended to be open-ended. UN Insiders now expect that Resolution 1373 will allow the UN to rise to a new level of empowerment. And in the longer term, the War on Terrorism will be used to justify vast new UN powers, in the name of combating a "global" threat.

The United Nations, then, instead of delivering world peace, has brought endless war for endless peace. This is because, as J. Reuben Clark and others warned long ago, the United Nations is designed and intended to bring about peace by military force. But only the peace of servitude can be imposed by warfare and terror. Such was the peace endured by the subjects of the Roman and Soviet empires. Such also is the nature of peace, UN-style, inflicted on the hapless residents of Iraq, Somalia, Bosnia, Serbia, Sierra Leone, Katanga, and many other countries. And such, in the longer run, will be the nature of global "peace" enforced by a future UN capable of imposing its will even on the United States, unless the UN system is dismantled.

6
Financial Chicanery

O nly a month before the conference at Dumbarton Oaks in 1944 described in Chapter 1, another secretive gathering took place at the Mount Washington Hotel in Bretton Woods, New Hampshire. Known nowadays as the "Bretton Woods conference," the gathering was formally called the United Nations Monetary and Financial Conference. Its purpose was to create an international system to control world finances complementing the United Nations framework for political and military control.

Much of what took place at Bretton Woods is still unknown. Records and transcripts of conference meetings are spotty, and participants were tightlipped about many of the proceedings. Representing the United States at Bretton Woods was a delegation led by Harry Dexter White, Roosevelt's Assistant Treasury Secretary (later unmasked as a Communist agent), who also attended the Dumbarton Oaks conference the following month. According to one Bretton Woods participant, Raymond Mikesell, who wrote a short memoir about the goings-on at the conference, White didn't consider himself accountable to any higher authority within the U.S. government:

> White sought to conduct his own foreign policy independently of the State Department. He dealt directly with foreign officials in Washington, and members of [U.S. embassy staffs overseas] secretly reported directly to White without going through their embassies.... On one occasion, while I was alone with him in his office, he dictated over the phone a long, top-secret State Department paper to a reporter.

At Bretton Woods, White presented a grand scheme: He wanted to create an organization to control international finance, destroy the financial independence of the nations of the world, and redistribute wealth from the rich to the poor countries. He called his scheme the International Monetary Fund, or IMF. The IMF was promoted as an instrument for international peace rather than international socialism since, as Mikesell admitted in his memoir, "the American public was not ready to embrace foreign aid, except to Allies in a common war. Assistance merely to induce countries to observe the rules of fair trade ... was not widely accepted. The war had, however, spawned broad support for international cooperation on behalf of peace and collective security. By tying Bretton Woods to the peace movement, the

Treasury Department, in collaboration with the rest of the administration, was able to elicit grass-roots support for the [International Monetary] Fund."

The IMF was foisted on Congress and the American public as a means of "stabilizing" international trade and currency exchange rates. Few people knew or cared what such phrases meant, but assumed that "stability" in any form would be a blessing in those chaotic times. But in reality, the IMF was intended to create *instability*, by sucking the world's poorer nations into total dependence on IMF loans, and by financially weakening the wealthy countries, especially the United States. The chaos created by such destabilization would allow the Insiders to integrate all countries, both rich and poor, into a single global economic and financial system.

The IMF is a sort of global money pool, to which countries "subscribe" by contributing a large "quota" determined by a complex and essentially meaningless formula. The quotas are then put into a common fund and are used to issue loans to deadbeat regimes, mostly in the so-called Third World. These loans are often issued at scandalously low interest rates, and are seldom if ever repaid — except by new loans extended to pay off the old. They do, however, come with strings attached: The IMF often imposes harsh conditions on debtor nations, requiring them to change their tax rates, heap more regulations on private enterprise, and so forth.

The IMF's lending money comes mostly from the world's richest countries, whose subscription quotas make up the lion's share of the IMF's reserves. The United States has contributed roughly $56 billion dollars, nearly one fifth of the total IMF reserves. This money comes from the American tax-paying public; government cannot spend any money that it doesn't first get by taxation in some form. Thanks to the IMF, then, tens of billions of taxpayer dollars are whisked out of the United States and into the coffers of corrupt, fiscally irresponsible regimes from Argentina to Indonesia.

Harry Dexter White's British counterpart at the Bretton Woods conference was economist and Fabian socialist John Maynard Keynes. Keynes, one of the 20th century's most influential advocates of the centrally planned economy, masterminded the other global financial organization to emerge from Bretton Woods, the International Bank for Reconstruction and Development, better known as the World Bank. Whereas the IMF specializes in loans to keep bankrupt economies and worthless currencies afloat, the World Bank pays out billions to Third World regimes for "infrastructure"-related boondoggles like dams and power plants. As with the IMF, the World Bank relies on United States taxpayer dollars for a sizable portion of its reserves.

It is astonishing that Americans would permit their government to tax them for the purpose of sending money to corrupt foreign regimes, but they do. Foreign aid in any form, whether laundered through international institutions like the IMF and the World Bank, or administered directly by the U.S. Agency for International Development (USAID) or some other U.S. government agency, is not authorized by the U.S. Constitution.

Government-administered foreign aid is morally reprehensible as well, whatever its defendants may say. Foreign aid is not charity, though it's often portrayed that way. Charity is given voluntarily to those genuinely in need. Foreign aid, by contrast, is taken forcibly from American taxpayers of every income level and given to those in poor countries who need it least — the corrupt elites who occupy the halls of government and corporate power. It therefore strengthens only those entrenched interests and individuals who are mostly responsible for their countries' hardships in the first place. Government foreign aid is nothing more than international welfare, and it has the same effect as its domestic counterpart. It encourages corruption and dependency — and dependency on the emerging global welfare state is exactly what its architects intended.

Foreign aid from the IMF and the World Bank not only creates a cycle of dependency and hopelessness among recipient nations, it also has adverse effects on donor nations like the United States. As we have seen, foreign aid is a form of naked government extortion. It frustrates and demoralizes American citizens, who see their hard-earned dollars sent abroad to benefit non-Americans contributing nothing to the well-being of the United States. Foreign aid saps the strength of our country by draining away wealth that is then redistributed overseas by unaccountable socialists at the IMF, the World Bank, and elsewhere. And, practiced long enough, the evil of foreign aid is finally tolerated by a citizenry weary of trying to stand up to corrupt and dishonest leaders who often make their own country's interests a very low priority.

Although the IMF and World Bank were created separately from the United Nations itself, both have since been merged into the United Nations system as affiliates. The creation of a single world financial system, including a world central bank and a single world currency, was the ultimate goal of the Insiders at Bretton Woods and remains a coveted objective. Originally, John Maynard Keynes tried to propose a single world currency, which he called the "bancor," but the world in 1944 wasn't yet ready for such a step. Instead, financial Insiders developed a long-range strategy to organize the world into regional economic blocs, with regional currencies and regional central banks that could later be consolidated into a single global entity.

The Insiders have already made considerable progress toward this goal. They began in Europe with the creation of the Common Market in the 1950s. Though many European countries were worried that the Common Market might endanger their sovereignty, they were assured by suave Insiders that the Common Market was nothing more than a "free trade" organization. But as the years passed and more countries joined the Common Market, the organization began to look and act more and more like a regional government. It changed its name first to European Economic Community (EEC), then to the European Community (EC), and finally to the European Union (EU), and agitated continuously for new powers. A European Central Bank was established in Frankfurt, Germany, in 1998, and on January 1, 2002 a new currency, the euro, was launched among the nations of the EU. National currencies, some of them centuries old, disappeared, including the franc, the mark, and the lira. EU dignitaries are now planning the next stage of what they call "integration" — that is, the destruction of the remnants of the sovereignty of Europe's once independent nations. In the works is a European Constitution, to give the force of law to the already-existing European parliament, council, and courts.

All of this came about as a result of Insider-controlled economic "integration." The Insiders understand that *eco-*

nomic union leads to *political* union. They plan to replicate the European model elsewhere, using regional economic blocs as the foundation for regional governments. Recently, a regional organization for Africa, the African Union or AU, was created. The AU, like the EU, will include a parliament, a council, a regional central bank, and an international court. Plans for a permanent rapid-reaction African peacekeeping force and a single continent-wide currency have also been announced.

In the Western Hemisphere, the Insiders are planning a regional authority that will encompass all of North, Central, and South America. The first stage of constructing such a regional economic regime was the creation of NAFTA, the North American Free Trade Agreement. NAFTA includes only the United States, Canada, and Mexico, but its effects have been enormous. As a result of the agreement, hundreds of U.S. companies have moved their operations south of the border, even as hundreds of thousands of Mexican immigrants, both legal and illegal, throng north across the Rio Grande in search of work.

But the underlying purpose of NAFTA, as many leaders in the United States and Mexico are well aware, is to pave the way for an EU-style superstate in the Americas. Mexican President Vicente Fox admitted as much in a speech given in Spain, where he assumed his remarks wouldn't be picked up by the American press:

> Eventually our long-range objective is to establish with
> the United States, but also with Canada, our other regional
> partner, an ensemble of connections and institutions similar
> to those created by the European Union.

NAFTA is just a piece of a much larger puzzle. The
Bush administration is now pushing for a hemisphere-wide
trade authority, the so-called FTAA (Free Trade Area of the
Americas). As with the Common Market and NAFTA, the
FTAA is being billed as a "free trade zone." Yet globalist
planners are already talking about a single pan-American
currency, which ought to trigger alarm bells for anyone
who has paid attention to events in Europe.

Caught between the hammer of global financial organizations like the IMF and the anvil of so-called "free trade"
arrangements like NAFTA, the United States is slowly but
steadily surrendering its economic and financial sovereignty
to international authorities. As a result, Americans are losing control of their taxpayer dollars, their economy, and
their national borders. The solution, though, is very simple:
We must withdraw from all multilateral financial and trade
organizations, and insist on setting our own trade policies
by negotiating individual treaties with individual nations.

We must also end all forms of government-administered foreign aid; both American taxpayers and the world's poor will be better off.

7
Courting Disaster

Our modern judicial system, with all its strengths and weaknesses, is the product of centuries of trial and error, so to speak. In feudal England, courts were created by kings as extensions of the monarchy. Over the centuries they evolved into more independent entities that began to act as a check against, rather than an extension of, the power of the crown. Provisions for rights such as trial by jury and habeas corpus, originating in English law, have become crucial defenses in the United States against the abuse of government power.

By the time of American independence, the great French political theorist Montesquieu had identified the judiciary as one of the three great divisions of government power. In order to safeguard the liberties of the people, Montesquieu argued, the judicial power must be separated from the other two powers of the state, the executive and the legislative. James Madison, who had studied Montesquieu, observed in *The Federalist*, No. 47, that "the accumulation of all powers, legislative, executive, and judiciary, in the same hands, whether of one, a few, or many, and whether hereditary, self-appointed, or elective, may justly be pronounced the very definition of tyranny."

Despite such advances, though, courts were often used as instruments of political policy. England's infamous Star Chamber, a court where all crimes that fell under the so-called "king's prerogative" were prosecuted, was used by a number of English monarchs, especially the tyrannical Henry VIII, to dispose of political enemies.

Although the Star Chamber was abolished in the 17th century, the British continued to use the courts as a weapon against American colonists. The Declaration of Independence accused King George of "depriving us, in many cases, of the benefits of trial by jury" and of "transporting us beyond the seas to be tried for pretended offenses." When America won her independence, the Founders, with memories of such abuses fresh in their minds, took pains to limit both the power of the judiciary and the ability of other branches of government to exploit the judicial branch for their own ends. As a result, the Constitution protects important freedoms like the privilege of a writ of habeas corpus and the right to a speedy and public trial by jury. At the same time, to guard against judicial collusion with the executive or legislative branch, the Supreme Court is granted considerable independence. However, the court is still subject to limits on its own power, since Congress is given the authority to limit its appellate jurisdiction.

The United Nations system, until recently, hasn't enjoyed much judicial power, except with occasional "war crimes" tribunals such as those used to prosecute the Serbs and the alleged participants in the Rwandan civil war. The original International Court of Justice, better known as the World Court, was created by the UN Charter specifically to hear disputes between states, and not to try individual citizens.

The new International Criminal Court or ICC, however, is an entirely different and far more dangerous organization. The ICC was created in 1998 under the so-called Rome Statute, a 300-page document hammered out over years of negotiations, and came into force in 2002.

The ICC is sometimes billed as an entity separate from the United Nations, but in reality, the UN has guided the creation of the ICC from the earliest drafts of the Rome Statute. Hans Corell, the UN's legal counsel, presided over the ceremony bringing the ICC into legal force. UN Secretary-General Kofi Annan verified, at an early ICC meeting, that "Mr. Corell and the Codification Division and the entire United Nations legal team have been working very hard to make sure that the Court comes into being." Like all other international treaties, the Rome Statute was registered under UN authority. It is therefore subordinate to the United

Nations, although it was created separately.

Described by one of its architects as "potentially the most important human rights institution created in 50 years," the International Criminal Court is not only another dangerous plank in the rising house of world order, it is also completely at odds with our centuries-old tradition of limited government and the separation of powers. In the words of Notre Dame law professor Charles Rice, the Rome Statute (the ICC treaty) "repudiates the Constitution, the Bill of Rights, and the Declaration of Independence, and cancels the 4th of July."

Like the United Nations itself, the ICC is designed to grow from a weak, largely symbolic organization into a global monstrosity with unlimited powers. As with the UN Security Council, the ICC is intended to be a law unto itself; Article 19 of the Rome Statute stipulates that "the Court shall satisfy itself that it has jurisdiction in any case brought before it." In other words, the ICC may decide to exercise jurisdiction wherever it pleases; no other branch of government, including the UN Security Council, can set limits on it.

With such an unlimited grant of power, it's not too surprising that the architects of the ICC have arrogantly decided that the court shall have jurisdiction over the entire planet, including nations that haven't ratified the ICC treaty. The ICC came into force on July 1, 2002, following ratification by the required 60 countries. The United States has so far refused to ratify the treaty, even though President Clinton signed it on December 30, 2000.

The International Criminal Court is everything the Founders feared about runaway judiciaries. It offers no guarantee of a speedy trial or a right to trial by jury. It recognizes no habeas corpus privilege. Accused criminals may be taken overseas for trial by foreign judges and tribunals; in practice, this might mean that American soldiers or other U.S. citizens accused of participating in "crimes against humanity" could be tried, convicted, and imprisoned in Europe or elsewhere, without the benefit of due process or any of the other rights and legal privileges guaranteed under American law. And the deliberately vague terminology used in the Rome Statute leaves the door wide open for many other misuses of power.

One hallmark of proper legal language is preciseness. Those who make and interpret law are keenly aware of how language may be manipulated to camouflage intent and to tease new meanings out of vaguely worded statutes. Good laws, therefore, are written in clear, unambiguous language, as a safeguard against human ingenuity. But the Insiders don't intend for the ICC to remain unchanged; they instead created an institution that, like the United Nations, is supposed to evolve over time. Therefore, the language of the

Rome Statute is ambiguous by design, to provide for broader and broader powers as the ICC grows in scope and influence.

For example, the Rome Statute's Article 5 defines as crimes within the ICC's jurisdiction "genocide," "crimes against humanity," "war crimes," and "aggression." For this last category, the Statute promises only that "the Court shall exercise jurisdiction over the crime of aggression once a provision is adopted ... defining the crime and setting out conditions under which the Court shall exercise jurisdiction with respect to this crime." The Court, in other words, may choose at some future time to define the crime of "aggression" any way it sees fit. In fact, it's difficult to imagine a crime in which "aggression" in some form doesn't play a part!

"Genocide," which for most of us conjures up images of Nazi pogroms and death camps, is defined in Section c of Article 6 as "causing serious bodily or mental harm" to members of any "national, ethnical, racial, or religious group." What might constitute "mental harm"? Under such a broad term, the ICC might claim jurisdiction over any act of so-called discrimination, from uttering racial slurs to condemning homosexuality from the pulpit.

"Crimes against humanity" are defined in part as "persecution against any identifiable group or collectivity based on political, racial, national, cultural, religious, gender ..., or other grounds that are universally recognized as impermissible under international law." Again, language of this sort could easily be used to justify prosecuting any act of discrimination, as defined in the modern, politically correct sense.

As for "war crimes," the Statute lists "intentionally directing attacks against the civilian population" and "against civilian objects," as well as "attacking or bombarding … towns, villages, dwellings or buildings which are undefended and which are not military objectives." On the basis of such "war crimes," U.S. military personnel could — and undoubtedly will, if the ICC has its way — be prosecuted for attacking, even accidentally, targets deemed civilian by biased foreign judges.

Finally, Article 123 of the Rome Statute provides an open-ended amendment process by which additional crimes can be added to the ICC's jurisdiction. In practical legal terms, this means that the ICC can be "upgraded" at any time in the future to have jurisdiction over any conceivable crime committed by anyone anywhere in the world.

ICC supporters argue that the court will never have such a reach, that it is intended primarily to prosecute international crimes too severe for national and local courts and laws to address. They insist that as long as conditions of so-called "complementarity" are observed by member states, there will be no need for the ICC to interfere with local jurisdictions. "Complementarity" means that all courts, at all levels, will abide by the standards of the ICC, and implies that nations will change their laws, where necessary, to recognize UN-defined crimes dealing with discrimination, the environment, employment, or whatever the issue of the moment happens to be. As Kofi Annan expressed it, "Countries that have established proper national criminal justice systems have nothing to fear from the Court.... But where national criminal justice systems are unwilling or unable to investigate or prosecute, the ICC will step in."

Whether the ICC exercises direct jurisdiction over Americans, or whether American courts and lawmakers merely kowtow to the ICC in changing U.S. statutes, the result will be the same: The ICC — run by foreign judges unaccountable to U.S. law and mostly biased against the United States and against American interests — will be allowed to override all American courts, including the U.S. Supreme Court.

None of this is at all far-fetched, given the UN's long record of anti-Americanism and the ultra-liberal, socialist attitudes of most of its members and supporters. The United States is widely resented and envied, especially among the leaders of the impoverished nations of Africa, Asia, and Latin America, who consider their poverty a consequence of American "imperialism" rather than their own misguided policies. UN member states, including regimes with dismal human rights records, routinely gang up on the United States, as when the United States was recently voted off the UN Human Rights Commission by the likes of Syria and Libya.

But beyond the politics is the principle, once again, of sovereignty. Regardless of the ICC's actual power to enforce its rulings, it is plainly being set up as a global Supreme Court, the judicial arm of the new world order, and completely unaccountable to any higher authority. Moreover, it's designed, like the rest of the UN-centered international system, to accrue power over time, so that future generations will certainly see American citizens hauled off for trial overseas, even if present-day politics won't allow that to happen. The only proper course is for America to reject not only the ICC, but to get out of the entire rotten UN system, which is founded on false and evil principles and largely run by people hostile to the United States

8
Peace and How to Achieve it

All of us want peace. We all want to live our lives and raise our children in a world free from the horrors of war. War destroys lives and property, visiting death and misery on civilians and combatants alike. Prolonged warfare hardens hearts, destroys laughter and innocence, overturns governments, and brings down economies. Without any doubt, war is the greatest of all scourges to afflict fallen man. It is therefore natural for men to want peace, to exhaust all possible recourses short of war before resorting to the ultimate solution, and to seek ways to encourage and prolong peace once it has been achieved.

Both the United Nations and its short-lived predecessor, the League of Nations, were forged in the fires of world war. In retrospect, with the benefit of more than a half century free from the kind of world-convulsing conflicts that our grandparents and our great-grandparents endured, it's easy to condemn the generation that allowed the United Nations to come into existence. We understand now, as few did in 1944, that the United Nations cannot fulfill its promise of world peace, nor did its founders create it to do so. But for a country and a people exhausted by world war, the siren song of the United Nations proved irresistible *because they could see no alternative.* In our day, many people still support, or at least tolerate, the UN, because they believe that the organization, despite all its flaws, is the best hope for world peace.

The United Nations, as we have seen, is an attempt to create a world government with the power to enforce peace, through military means if necessary. *But peace by military force is simply another name for war.* In the words of J. Reuben Clark, "the [UN] Charter provides for force to bring peace, but such use of force is itself war."

Let's consider some of the fallacies in circulation about the United Nations before showing the alternative, proper road to peace:

Fallacy: *Just as enforceable law is necessary to maintain peace among individuals, with government as the enforcing agent, so enforceable international law, implemented by international or world government, is necessary to regulate the relationships among separate nations.* The founding legal and political thinkers of the modern era, from Grotius and Vattel to the American Founding Fathers, believed not in international law as it is now understood but in the law of nations. The latter term refers primarily to the "laws of nature and nature's God" applied to sovereign nations, and also includes unenforceable, man-made treaties which were understood to be the international equivalent of gentleman's agreements. The law of nations was not regarded as enforceable by any man-made authority superior to the separate, sovereign nations themselves. Sovereign countries may invoke the law of nations as justification for defending their rights against aggressor nations, and may even sign treaties to commit themselves to an agreed-upon course of action. But sovereign countries may also violate the law of nations and any treaties they have voluntarily entered into, and are amenable directly only to God for such acts.

On the other hand, the modern idea of *enforceable* international law presupposes international or world government — which is precisely what the UN-centered new world order is becoming. Therefore, all arguments in favor of enforceable international law are in fact arguments for world government and an end to national sovereignty. But to end national sovereignty, as we saw in Chapter 2, is to deny men their most fundamental God-given collective right — the right of forming a collective force or government completely independent of any other authority — and to effectively repudiate the Declaration of Independence and the U.S. Constitution.

Fallacy: *Without a global authority, we can never have world peace. The United Nations might not be perfect, but it's our last, best chance to achieve permanent peace. At least at the United Nations, countries can air their differences.* True world peace cannot be attained by military force; the "tranquility of servitude," to use Samuel Adams' memorable phrase, must not be confused with lasting peace. Peace is best achieved under conditions of national sovereignty, in which nations are free to negotiate with each other. A "forum" for airing grievances publicly and involving the entire "international community" is about as effective as a bickering couple involving the entire neighborhood in their problems. As with married couples, so with nations: The best way to resolve disputes is through quiet, patient, personal diplomacy.

Fallacy: *We can't have peace in a world of sovereign nations, where every country is armed to the teeth. The only route to peace is disarmament under some kind of global authority.* This argument assumes that weapons cause wars, and is similar to the mistaken belief, used to justify the disarmament of U.S. citizens, that guns cause crimes. But both crimes and wars are caused, not by weapons, but by our fallible human natures. As the Apostle James put it, "From whence come wars and fighting among you? Come they not hence, even of your lusts that war in your members? Ye lust, and have not: ye kill, and desire to have, and cannot obtain: ye fight and war, yet ye have not, because ye ask not." (James 4: 1-2). No form of government, including world government, can change human nature.

Moreover, because of man's imperfect nature, every effort should be made to limit, not increase, the power of government. Good government — the best that mortal man can devise, at any rate — is diffuse, limited, and primarily local. Bad government — that which will tend to bring out the worst in man by giving him maximum incentives to abuse power — is concentrated, unlimited, and encompasses within its jurisdiction the largest possible amount of territory and number of souls. World government, and especially a world government with the power and will to disarm the entire planet, will necessarily be of the latter kind.

In reality, the champions of so-called "disarmament" aren't proposing that we rid the world of all military weapons and beat all our swords into plowshares. Instead, advocates of disarmament support placing all military forces, including nuclear weapons, under a single global regime. Disarmament, then, isn't about eliminating weapons but about monopolizing them.

Fallacy: *But we'll have world federalism, replicating on a global scale the federal model of the United States system, and not totalitarian global tyranny. Surely all Americans ought to support such an arrangement!* In the first place, even if a federal world government were the aim of the Insiders, it wouldn't be feasible. Federalism only works, on an extended scale, among a people of similar customs, language, culture, and values. As John Jay wrote in *The Federalist*, No. 2:

Providence has been pleased to give this one connected country to one united people — a people descended from the same ancestors, speaking the same language, professing the same religion, attached to the same principles of government, very similar in their manners and customs....

All large "multi-ethnic" modern states — the Soviet Union, Indonesia, and India come to mind — have resorted to authoritarian or outright totalitarian government to maintain order. Even many small states, such as Israel, Yugoslavia, Great Britain, Sri Lanka, and Rwanda, have been unable to deal with ethnic, religious, and language differences without bloodshed and police state measures. A global government by any name would have to be totalitarian to hold together — strong enough to crush by force any dissenting faction or group, ruthless enough to terrorize people into submission, and pervasive enough to keep tabs on the entire planet.

But in truth, as this book has already shown, the architects of the UN were not aiming for "world federalism," except in name. They were socialists and Communists, and no more believed in limited government than in national sovereignty. Any future world government under the UN will look more like the former Soviet Union — in which a fiction of separate "republics" was maintained under an all-powerful central authority — than any limited "federal" arrangement.

Fallacy: *We live in an interconnected world, and we can't withdraw and revert to isolationism. Like it or not, things that happen all over the world, and especially in areas of strategic interest, affect us, so we must stay engaged.* "Isolationist" is a favorite label the Insiders use to discredit their opponents. In reality, the United States has never been isolationist. At the time of America's founding, for example, John Jay, in *The Federalist*, No. 4, could already cite trade not only with the nations of Europe, but with China and India as well. The foreign policy advocated by the Founding Fathers, and adhered to by subsequent U.S. administrations for several generations, was not isolationism but *non-interventionism*. Non-interventionism, simply put, is the old virtue of minding one's own business applied to foreign affairs.

It's true that we live in an interconnected world — as

far as the private sector is concerned. Trade has ever been the tie that binds nations together, as private citizens exchange goods and services across international boundaries. But trade has flourished for centuries, with sovereign states signing bilateral trade agreements and granting each other's citizens permission to enter their sovereign territories, transact business, and even establish residency.

Trade wars and tariffs (taxes on imported goods) are often portrayed as evils that only an international authority can eliminate. But in truth, tariffs, which were once the largest source of federal revenues, are one of the least objectionable forms of taxation, because they are the among the least intrusive. As for trade "wars," the term is more severe than the reality. Disagreements between nations over trade policies sometimes lead to tit-for-tat tariff hikes and restrictions on imports. However, nations usually resolve trade disputes without resorting to shooting war.

Fallacy: *What about our military and strategic interests? Doesn't the existence of modern weapons of mass destruction, jet aircraft, and ICBMs — not to mention terrorism — make military non-interventionism downright dangerous, as well as strategically unwise? And how else can we defend our interests overseas, such as the Middle Eastern oil fields, if we aren't willing to maintain overseas bases and cooperate with the United Nations in waging war abroad?*

Questions such as these are used to rationalize the broader doctrine of military interventionism, a subject on which honest men can and do disagree. But they cannot justify the particular kind of interventionism in which the United Nations has involved the American military: multilateral (i.e., involving many countries) military intervention in defense not of American interests but those of the "international community." Sometimes the interests invoked by the United Nations may appear to coincide with our own (e.g., "peacekeeping" in the Middle East), but more often they do not. No one can give a shred of evidence to show how American national interests are furthered by our UN-brokered entanglement in hot spots like Yugoslavia and Somalia. In essence, there's a huge difference between unilateral American military activities overseas — such as the deployment of naval, air and land forces in international waters and on overseas bases, to defend national interests — and sending our forces willy-nilly around the globe, often under foreign command, to further the purposes of the United Nations.

Fallacy: *The U.S. president needs UN authority to deploy troops overseas and to commit forces for collective security.* The U.S. Constitution gives the president very limited war powers. He is the commander-in-chief of the U.S. armed forces, but that grant of authority does not include license to start wars or deploy U.S. forces whenever and wherever he pleases, whether in the name of the United Nations or any other extra-constitutional authority. Congress is given the sole authority to declare war, a power that would be completely meaningless if the Founders had intended the president to use the military at his personal discretion, like a monarch.

Involvement in the United Nations has been directly responsible for the erosion of one of the key checks and balances in our federal government, the constitutionally mandated division of war powers between the president and Congress. President Harry S. Truman stared down congressional opposition and sent our troops into the Korean War without a congressional declaration of war — the first time a U.S. president dared to do so. To justify his action, Truman claimed that the new UN Charter gave him the necessary authority to commit U.S. troops to the Korean "police action," regardless of what Congress thought about it. From that day to this, U.S. presidents, following Truman's lead, have sent U.S. troops into combat in Vietnam, Iraq, Yugoslavia, Somalia, Panama, and now Afghanistan, without a declaration of war and under the direct or indirect authority of the United Nations.

Fallacy: *In this modern age, we now have a global com-*

mons containing "global public goods"— the air we breathe, the oceans, outer space, the electromagnetic spectrum, etc. — that all of us use (and sometimes abuse) and that therefore must be regulated by a global authority. This argument has been used to justify everything from global taxation to UN regulation of shipping lanes and seabed mining. It's really just a more sophisticated way of making the old claim that "we're all one world, so we should have one world government." And, for reasons already given, world government cannot work except as a totalitarian regime. The fact that some parts of the world, like the oceans and the atmosphere, have always been treated as international doesn't mean that they must be brought under the control of an international governing body. Discerning men have always understood and believed that the world as a whole belongs to its Creator, not to His human creations. Keeping this fact in mind helps us to remember that there is, after all, an authority higher than any earthly government. Neglect of this point will lead us to conclude, falsely, that the Earth by rights belongs to "us" — as manifested by the "international community" and the United Nations.

Fallacy: *Even if everything you say about the UN is true in theory, it will never actually become a world government, because world government can't work. The American people would never permit the United Nations to "take over" completely, so there is no point in making so much fuss about a paper tiger.* Of all the misstatements that have been made about the United Nations, this one is surely the most pernicious. As we have already shown, the United Nations is designed to become a world government by installment plan. The United Nations is evil not because blue-helmeted troops are rampaging on American soil, enforcing a global police state right now. It's evil in principle, and therefore must be done away with because evil principles, sooner or later, will produce evil consequences. James Madison understood the long-term danger of yielding to false principles when he said:

It is proper to take alarm at the first experiment on our liberties. We hold this prudent jealousy to be the first duty of citizens and one of the noblest characteristics of the late Revolution. The freemen of America did not wait till usurped power had strengthened itself by exercise and entangled the question in precedents. They saw all the consequences in principle, and they avoided the consequences by denying the principle.

Madison put his finger on one of the cardinal problems with politics: People often fail to anticipate, or willfully ignore, the long-term effects of misguided policies. They live for today, so to speak, never considering the effect that today's flawed policies may have on generations yet unborn. Few Americans foresaw, when they permitted their government to amend the Constitution in 1913 to provide for a permanent, graduated income tax, that America would end up with the oppressive tax system of today. They were asked to trust their government, which promised never to tax any but the very rich, and only at a very low rate. Only a few far-sighted individuals foresaw that the income tax would grow into a monstrosity. Those prescient few perceived the principles and the purposes behind the proposal, and correctly forecast that the income tax would burden future generations with a yoke that would be difficult to remove.

Similarly, a totalitarian world government, with comprehensive powers of global taxation, police, military, surveillance, and every other type of regulation, is difficult for many people to imagine. We are willing to flirt with the United Nations because we see the UN only as it is, not as what it is intended to become. We fail to understand the purposes of its founders and the false principles that the UN was created to advance. And because the UN accumulates power slowly, gradually, and stealthily, we refuse to awaken to the threat.

Fallacy: *With all its imperfections, the United Nations still is dedicated to a noble purpose. Therefore, rather than throw it out completely, we should reform it so that it will still serve some useful purposes, without being a threat to our sovereignty.* This line of argument has seduced many who otherwise oppose the United Nations. But it's as flawed as the rest. The United Nations cannot be reformed because it is based on evil principles, and was founded by evil men for evil purposes, as we have seen. Many of those who created and who sustain the UN enjoy positions of power and influence within the U.S. government. These individuals are completely dedicated to delivering the United States into world government — regardless of the wishes of the American people.

For the United Nations to truly live up to its defined mission, our Constitution and Declaration of Independence would have to be scrapped. Simply put, the United Nations cannot achieve its objectives without totalitarian world government. Evil cannot be reformed; it must be shunned, or it will triumph.

Despite fallacies like these, the quest for peace continues. How can peace be achieved, if not through an international body like the United Nations? This is another loaded question, since, before trying to answer it, we must clarify: Peace for *whom*? World peace is something quite different from peace where the United States of America is concerned. The only kind of peace our government has any constitutional authority to be concerned with is our own. Our federal government is authorized to negotiate treaties, to "provide for the common defense," to "establish *domestic* tranquility," to suppress internal rebellions, and, when necessary, to wage war against hostile powers. It isn't authorized to enforce peace between hostile third-party nations or to provide American servicemen to police foreign lands in a state of civil unrest, like Bosnia and Somalia. Simply put, the Constitution nowhere authorizes the U.S. government to be the world's policeman, or to try to solve all of the world's problems. This was what prompted John Quincy Adams to say that "[America] is the well-wisher to the freedom and independence of all. She is the champion and vindicator only of her own."

For many generations, America was seen, both by her citizens and by people abroad, as a haven from the problems plaguing the rest of the world. Therefore, deliberately immersing ourselves in the problems of religion, race, and historical animosity that beset much of the rest of the world is unnecessary and foolish. Recall that George Washington, in his Farewell Address, warned America against needlessly "quit[ting] our own to stand upon foreign ground."

Another perceptive critic of American interventionism,

Yale University professor and essayist William Graham Sumner, writing at the time of the Spanish-American War, pointed out:

> [E]xpansion and imperialism are at war with the best traditions, principles, and interests of the American people, and they will plunge us into a network of difficult problems and political perils.... The people ... who now want us to break out, warn us against the terrors of "isolation." Our ancestors all came here to isolate themselves from the social burdens and inherited errors of the old world.... What we are doing is that we are abandoning this blessed isolation to run after a share in the trouble.

The best way to ensure peace for ourselves is to mind our own business and avoid any involvement in foreign conflicts that do not concern us. We must understand that we cannot do many things, even with all our technology, wealth, and military might. We can no more change the disposition of men to make war than we can guarantee an end to pain, sickness, natural disasters, or any of the other trials and tribulations that crop up in our imperfect world.

At the same time, we can use a very powerful tool to discourage war among the nations of the world, a tool that the Insiders would have us ignore: the power of example.

John Winthrop, the Pilgrim leader who become governor of the Massachusetts Bay colony, told his followers that "we shall be as a City upon a Hill. The eyes of all people are upon us." From that day to this, Americans have set an example for the rest of the world. We have become the world's wealthiest and most powerful nation, a dominant influence not only economically and militarily but culturally as well. People all over the world listen to our music, watch our movies, copy our methods of doing business, and learn our language. No nation in all of human history has enjoyed such worldwide prestige, power, and influence as the modern United States of America.

But other countries do not imitate our ways because they're forced to. They do so because they want to become like us. They see the fruits of our civilization and want to partake of them.

To a lesser degree, this same principle has applied to politics. Much of the world has adopted some form of representative government with a written constitution. While most such governments remain oppressive and inadequate when compared to our own, they nevertheless are mostly attempts to imitate the American form of government. Many countries have changed their laws to permit religious freedom, freedom of the press, and other basic rights that Americans have taken for granted for centuries.

The important point is that people learn best by example and by experience. We love to read books about successful men and women, for example, because we hope to learn how to replicate their success.

Peace is no different from any other desirable thing. If we want the world to be a more peaceful place, we must be peaceful ourselves. If we wish to avoid being offended by other countries, we must avoid giving offense. As a nation we should be slow to anger, using war only as a last resort.

Unfortunately, under the influence of the United Nations we have done precisely the opposite. We have become a very warlike nation, quick to rise to the slightest provocation, real or perceived. We willingly send our ships, our planes, and our fighting men to the far corners of the globe to enforce UN edicts. We have made many enemies across the world as a result. Instead of peace, we are advocating warfare and the willingness to use unlimited force to solve problems. Should we then be surprised when the rest of the world follows our example?

We will never live in a perfect world. We will never even be able to guarantee world peace, but we can encourage it by example. If we maintain a strong military to protect our freedom and independence, we will discourage would-be aggressors. If we avoid resorting to open war except when left with no other choice, we will set a powerful example for other nations, who will see the benefits of peace and will follow our lead.

9
The Solution

Our nearly 60-year-long involvement with the United Nations system — the entire military, legal, financial, and social international octopus — has brought us nothing but trouble. The UN has involved us in wars, sapped our financial and economic resources, worked to change our laws, and gradually undermined our national sovereignty. Instead of peace, we've gotten almost incessant war. Instead of international financial stability, we've gotten chaos. And instead of independence, we've gotten the false promises of what internationalists like to call "interdependence" — dependence by another name. In the UN's "interdependent" world, scores of countries are literally dependent upon the United States for military protection, foreign aid, and jobs created by U.S. companies building plants in countries otherwise almost incapable of creating jobs for their own impoverished, overtaxed, and tightly-controlled citizenries. At the same time, the United States itself has become dangerously dependent on Middle East oil, a relationship that has sparked conflict and war over the last couple of decades.

The Solution

Our modern "interdependent" world is not a sponta-
neous outgrowth of natural economic and political forces.
It's largely an artificial creation of the United Nations system and the Insiders who manage it. Their goal — an international system of weakened, dependent nations clinging to
the UN system for life support, as a prelude to outright
world government — is already taking shape. Once-inde-
pendent nations like Argentina (which in the early 20th century had one of the world's strongest economies) are now
completely dependent on IMF-administered international
aid. Thanks in large part to so-called "free trade" agreements such as GATT and NAFTA, the U.S. has become
dependent on cheap immigrant labor, while sending much
of its manufacturing sector overseas. Many countries in
Europe and Asia have lost the will to provide for their own
national defense, because these countries know they can
depend upon U.S. and UN forces for protection.

But the UN system itself is not yet independent either.
It relies for sustenance on the one source of health and vigor
that can keep it alive: the United States of America, with all
of its military, political, and economic clout. Like a biological parasite, the United Nations has fastened itself onto a
larger, more powerful organism, relying for its continued
survival on tapping the vitality of its host. The UN parasite
depends for its military power on American weaponry, tech-

nology, military intelligence, and personnel, especially in places like the Balkans and the Middle East. The UN's international financial system is heavily supported by money extracted from U.S. taxpayers. The UN's headquarters are located on U.S. soil. And the United Nations derives much of its operating funds — the money with which it pays for its lavish East River headquarters and numerous regional offices, as well as the inflated salaries of its thousands of employees — from generous American membership dues, which only recently, under the second Bush administration, were paid in full, including millions of dollars in past dues.

Given this dependency relationship, we might be tempted to ignore the United Nations threat. It is, after all, weaker than we are. But besides being weaker than their hosts, malignant parasites have another characteristic: Over time, they drain their host of strength, and finally overwhelm it, leaving only a dead or dying shell. This is the real danger. The UN parasite has already weakened us considerably, while gaining strength itself. It has siphoned billions of dollars from the United States economy. It has helped to sustain regimes, like the People's Republic of China and Fidel Castro's Cuba, that are self-described enemies of the United States. It has gradually gained the military power to crush countries like Iraq. It is quickly acquiring legal, judicial, and police powers over private citizens across the globe, and is working steadily to gain the power to levy taxes as well. If such trends are allowed to continue, the parasite will surely become stronger than the host. The UN eventually will wrench itself free from depending entirely on its weakened host, the United States, and begin to exercise direct authority over it and all other nations.

This has been the goal of UN planners and Insiders for decades. A shocking Kennedy-era document entitled *Freedom From War: The United States Program for General and Complete Disarmament in a Peaceful World* calls for gradually strengthening the UN military forces, even as member states are persuaded to disarm themselves, until "no state would have the military power to challenge the progressively strengthened U.N. Peace Force." Under such an outcome, "states would retain only those forces, non-nuclear armaments, and establishments required for the purpose of maintaining internal order" and "the manufacture of armaments would be prohibited except for those of agreed types and quantities to be used by the U.N. Peace Force and those required to maintain internal order. All other armaments would be destroyed or converted to peaceful purposes."

While *Freedom From War* was released more than 40 years ago, the policy goals it recommends have not changed. Most of the seeming contradictions and absurdities of

American foreign policy can be explained in terms of one very simple goal: empowering the United Nations. The more than decade-long dance with Iraq's Saddam Hussein makes sense only if the observer understands that the underlying purpose — of the Gulf War, the UN "weapons inspection" regime and trade embargo imposed on Iraq, and the "no-fly zones" and intermittent military action against Baghdad throughout the '90s and into the next decade — is to legitimize and to empower the United Nations. Who has been the beneficiary of the "containment" of Iraq? Not the United States, which has poured vast sums of money into patrolling the skies of Iraq and setting up new bases across the Middle East. This activity has resulted in increased anti-American sentiment across much of the Muslim world, and a Middle East that's more violent and unstable than ever. Nor have the oppressed people of Iraq benefited; it is they who suffer under both Saddam Hussein's appalling police state and the UN embargo.

Only the United Nations has benefited from the long-term military and economic campaign against Iraq. Its power and prestige grew enormously, thanks to the Gulf War and the decade-long UN-mandated embargo and intermittent military campaign that followed. The same could be said of the Balkan crisis, which led to several UN- and NATO-directed wars, a permanent UN military presence in the volatile region, and a convenient pretext to create a UN "war crimes tribunal" for arresting and prosecuting Serbian "war criminals."

Now we have the "War on Terrorism," which has been a UN project from the start. The defining authority for the war on terrorism is not a U.S. congressional declaration of war, or a piece of legislation like the USA PATRIOT Act. It is, as already noted, UN Security Council Resolution 1373, issued on September 28, 2001, which sets the conditions under which UN member states (that is, everybody) will conduct the fight against terrorism. The longer the war on terrorism continues, the stronger the United Nations is likely to become. Each new Security Council resolution and each new UN-coordinated military action in the war on terrorism will further strengthen the precedents giving the UN more and more jurisdiction over international affairs.

The United Nations system is gaining strength on many fronts besides military activity. An aggressive new international campaign is underway to give the United Nations direct global taxing authority. Proponents of the International Criminal Court continue to pressure the U.S. government to acknowledge the court's jurisdiction. In many respects, the UN is already a world government: It is the most powerful authority on the African continent; it enjoys a decisive presence in the Middle East and on the

Korean peninsula, and, via NATO, it is the de facto supreme military authority in Europe. For hundreds of millions of people, the new world order has already arrived.

What is the solution? As far as the United States is concerned, the solution is to starve the parasite — that is, to get the United States out of the UN system entirely and banish the organization from American soil. Without the sustaining nourishment of American taxpayer dollars and military forces, the United Nations will soon wither and die like its predecessor, the League of Nations.

This is the only answer; no half-measures will do. The United Nations cannot be reformed, since it was designed for purposes that are completely incompatible with American liberties. Moreover, its organization is corrupt, riddled with Communists, Third World despots, and other elements hostile to the United States.

But getting the United States out of the United Nations is easier said than done. Millions of Americans have already awakened to the peril of UN membership. Millions more resent the deployment of thousands of American troops overseas in feckless peacekeeping missions. Most of us are sick of being overtaxed, and don't take kindly to our tax dollars being shipped overseas to sustain oppressive regimes in Africa, Asia, and Latin America. Yet despite the fact that most Americans are opposed to the policies of the new world order, the United States remains firmly entangled in the UN system. Taxes continue to rise, American troops continue to be dispersed across the globe to defend the interests of the United Nations, and the power of international institutions like the ICC and the IMF continues to expand.

Why do the United Nations and the entire international system of emerging world government continue to grow, if so many Americans are opposed to it? One word sums up the reason for this seeming contradiction: organization. The Insiders are well organized and well financed, and have been for generations. They have a clear plan of action, with well-defined goals and a strategy to achieve them.

In contrast, most opposition to the United Nations is unorganized. Public awareness of the UN and its real agenda has never been higher, thanks to hundreds of talk shows filling the airwaves with anti-UN talk, and numerous web sites offering anti-UN books, articles, and other materials. The Internet and other media, if used responsibly, can be powerful tools, but none of these activities by itself will yield any concrete results, because, absent organization and a plan of action, none of them has any leverage to move the machinery of power. Talk, as we all know, is cheap.

A wise English statesman, Edmund Burke, once warned that "when bad men combine, the good must associate; else they will fall one by one, an unpitied sacrifice in a contemptible struggle." What Burke meant is that organization can only be resisted and overcome by organization. Therefore, the organized drive to empower the United Nations system and the new world order must have organized opposition. If we are to get the United States out of the UN system, we must have an organized campaign.

Fortunately, there is one organization working to get us out of the United Nations. The John Birch Society, using a focused nationwide campaign aptly named "*Get US out! of the UN*," is supplying the leadership needed to rid the United States of the United Nations. The campaign is the only one of its kind, and has been in motion for several decades. Recently, the effort has been intensified, to keep up with the tide of current events. The "*Get US out! of the UN*" campaign now features a nationwide network of "Get US out!" committees and an array of new tools, including pamphlets, magazines, and this book. We encourage all concerned citizens to get involved in this undertaking, the only *organized* effort to have our nation withdraw from the United Nations, while we still have the freedom to do so.

Getting involved in a drive to get out of the United Nations might seem too tall a task for ordinary citizens. The United Nations system is influential and well-entrenched, and the people and interests who defend the UN will certainly meet any serious campaign to get rid of it with every weapon in their odious arsenal. Any ordinary American might appear puny and powerless to make a difference in a conflict of such magnitude.

Regardless of such concerns, every patriotic American must get involved in this fight. As Edmund Burke reminded us, "nobody made a greater mistake than he who did nothing because he could only do a little." The John Birch Society's "Get US out!" campaign will provide the organization and the leadership necessary to win this struggle. If enough decent, ordinary Americans do their part in support of an organized effort — even if it's only "a little" — the United Nations will speedily end up in the dustbin of history, where it belongs.

Afterword:
For further reading

No one could hope to do justice to a subject as vast as the United Nations in a book of this length. Volumes have been written on all of the topics covered in these pages. The following books will help the reader learn more about the United Nations system, including many aspects not covered in this very brief introduction to the subject.

The reader should first become more thoroughly acquainted with the United Nations as a whole, and the best resource for this is William F. Jasper's book, *The United Nations Exposed* (The John Birch Society, 2001). Mr. Jasper, a longtime investigative reporter for *The New American* magazine, has attended many UN conferences and written many articles and two major books on the subject. He is probably the foremost living critic of the United Nations. His book may appear formidable to some readers, but a careful reading of his copiously documented chapters will give the serious student a comprehensive introduction to every facet of the UN system.

The best account of the Dumbarton Oaks conference is

Afterword

Robert C. Hildebrand's book *Dumbarton Oaks: The Origins of the United Nations and the Search for Postwar Security* (University of North Carolina Press, 1990).

The best and most concise modern book on the topic of sovereignty is Cornell University professor Jeremy Rabkin's *Why Sovereignty Matters* (AEI Press, 1998). Dr. Rabkin's prose is refreshingly clear, and his treatment of the topic of sovereignty is intended for a general audience. For historical documents about sovereignty, Emmerich de Vattel's *The Law of Nations* has been translated into English, but is out of print. This almost forgotten book is challenging but well worth reading, because it was the major inspiration for the Founding Fathers' foreign policy. For the views of the Founders themselves, *The Federalist Papers*, which every student of the U.S. Constitution and of limited government ought to read, is an indispensable source. It makes clear the ideas behind the founding of the American republic (what is so often inaccurately called — by those who fail to comprehend the Founding Fathers and their intentions — an "experiment" in limited government). The most important founding-era statement on American foreign policy per se is Washington's Farewell Address, a must-read for anyone wishing to be truly informed about the original intent of the Founding Fathers.

Reliable works on the Insiders are hard to find, because

so much that has been written on the subject indulges in hysterical speculation. Gary Allen's classic work *None Dare Call It Conspiracy* was one of the first sober works alerting modern Americans to the organized conspiracy waging war against our freedom. John McManus' pocket-sized book *The Insiders* (The John Birch Society, 1995) is an overview of the Insiders and their activities in the United States government over the past generation. James Perloff's *Shadows of Power* (Western Islands, 1988) deals specifically with the Council on Foreign Relations and its long history of influence. For the perspective of an Insider who decided to "tell all," however mercenary his motives, Dr. Carroll Quigley's two pivotal works *The Anglo-American Establishment* and *Tragedy and Hope* are indispensable sources. The latter is a turgid volume more than 1,300 pages in length, chock full of surprisingly candid details on the activities of the Insiders. For the determined reader, Quigley is truly an eye-opener.

Every informed American should read the UN Charter carefully, and ponder its meaning. Another important UN document that gives insight into the philosophy of the United Nations is the UN's Universal Declaration of Human Rights, adopted by the UN General Assembly in 1948. Parents should also read carefully the UN Declaration of the Rights of the Child, adopted in 1959, and consider its bearing on parental rights, among other things. Each of these UN documents is readily available on the Internet.

An interesting early perspective on the UN by an Insider who was one of America's most prominent men in the mid-20th century is *War or Peace* by John Foster Dulles. The book is fairly brief but dull reading, and gives a glimpse into the mindset of the men who created the United Nations.

The various UN-brokered wars of the 20th, and now, the 21st, centuries, are a matter of open historical record and the subject of nightly news broadcasts. G. Edward Griffin's *The Fearful Master* (Western Islands, 1964) provided an early look at the United Nations, with a detailed exposé of the UN's war against Katanga. Mark Bowden's *Black Hawk Down: A Story of Modern War* (Atlantic Monthly, 1999) is a brutally detailed account of the United States fiasco in Somalia.

Good books on international finance are hard to find. The IMF's own web site gives very detailed information about how the IMF works. G. Edward Griffin's book *The Creature From Jekyll Island* (American Opinion, 1994), while primarily concerned with the Federal Reserve System, has some very useful material on the IMF and foreign aid.

William Norman Grigg's two valuable books, *Freedom on the Altar* (American Opinion, 1995) and *Global Gun Grab* (The John Birch Society, 2001), deal with two important topics not covered in this book, the UN's religious and social agenda and the UN's growing interest in civilian disarmament (that is, confiscation of privately owned firearms), respectively.

Finally, every American should be intimately familiar with both the Declaration of Independence and the U.S. Constitution, both of which show that our nation's very existence is utterly incompatible with membership in the UN-centered new world order. If these two documents alone were more widely read and understood, the United Nations would have lost U.S. support and been disbanded a long time ago.

Index

About The Author

Steve Bonta has written extensively for *The New American* magazine as both a writer and contributing editor. In that capacity he had the opportunity, in March 2002, of traveling to Monterey, Mexico, to cover the UN's conference on Financing for Development. More recently, Mr. Bonta was appointed Director of Robert Welch University. Mr. Bonta received his B.A. from Penn State University in 1989 in Comparative Literature, his M.A. in linguistics from Brigham Young University in 1996, and is now finishing a PhD in the same subject from Cornell University.

Mr. Bonta has traveled widely and has lived abroad in South America, Asia, and Europe, and is proficient in a number of foreign languages. He and his wife of twelve years, Karylee, live in Appleton, Wisconsin.

About The John Birch Society

Since 1958, members of The John Birch Society have led the drive to restore constitutional limitations on government, preserve our nation's independence, and uphold the principles that have made our country the envy of mankind.

The John Birch Society is a nationwide information and action organization, consisting of thousands of ordinary Americans — Americans who have a deep, personal commitment to preserving freedom for future generations. Members inform themselves and others, and then work together to preserve freedom and bring about change in national policy where it is needed. For more information please visit www.jbs.org.

Get US out! of the United Nations

Join with thousands of other Americans working to *Get US out!* of the United Nations. Take the action steps outlined at *www.getusout.org* and order our *"Get US out! Starter Kit"* ($9.95 + shipping and handling) to carry out a proven strategy to increase your effectiveness and influence. Every individual can make a difference in the battle to preserve freedom.

www.getusout.org

Inside The United Nations
a critical look at the UN

is available in single or discounted quantities.

Quantity	Price/Book
1	.$4.95
10	.$3.95
30	.$2.95
90 + ...	.$2.00

Order online at www.getusout.org

or call 1-800-JBS-USA1

or write P.O. Box 8040, Appleton, WI 54912

Order Subtotal	Standard Shipping	Rush Shipping
$0-19.99	$3.00	$8.00
$20.00-49.99	$7.50	$12.50
$50.00-99.99	$10.00	$15.00
$100.00 +	$12.50	$17.50

Standard 4-14 business days, Rush 3-7 business days,
no P.O. boxes, Alaska/Hawaii add $10.00.
Wisconsin residents add 5% sales tax.